ALAN BATES

WIDE AWAKE

By Royal Appointment

(PHPA DHP Acc.) FESH

Dear Gary
To Good Old Times

Alan x

OCTOBER 2018

Sincere thanks to Dr Alan Roberts and to Martin Higgins, author of the novel, Human+, available on Amazon, for their assistance in producing this book.

Cover design Robert Doyle www.robdoyle.co.uk

Cover images, Tony Roberts LSWPP
www.tonyrobertsphotography.co.uk

ISBN-13: 978-1511936866

Other books available from the author,

Hypnotic Star published 2002. ISBN 0-9541111-1-7

For further information about the author, the following websites are listed below:

www.alanbates.tv

www.alanbatestherapiesuk.tv

www.facebook.com/alanbates.tv

www.facebook.com/alanbatesinmalta

Email info@alanbates.tv

TO MY CHILDREN,

ATLANTA, ESTELLE, JAY, KEIRA & AMBER BATES

"**THERE IS ONLY ONE THING WORSE THAN BEING TALKED ABOUT, AND THAT IS NOT BEING TALKED ABOUT.**"

OSCAR WILDE

"**THERE IS ONLY ONE TRUE HAPPINESS IN LIFE, TO LOVE AND BE LOVED.**"

GEORGE SAND

THE NEUROTIC BUILDS CASTLES IN THE SKY, THE PSYCHOTIC LIVES IN THEM AND THE PSYCHIATRIST COLLECTS THE RENT.

ACKNOWLEDGEMENTS

A big hearty thanks goes out to my Mum and Dad who have stood by me from my early nurture to present times. Through personal experience, I know that watching your children grow is one of the greatest pleasures in life and I have been very fortunate to have such good parents.

My younger brothers, Gary and John Bates, who have had to put up with me for all these years, but have added brotherly love, fun and happiness to my very crazy world.

To all the dear friends, associates and acquaintances throughout the world (all named in the Meeting of Souls chapter) who, over the years, have enriched my life with great experiences.

To my wonderful children that I love so dearly – Atlanta, Estelle, Jay, Keira and Amber Bates – who have fulfilled my life greatly. And, to my yet unknown future generations, who are the reason for sharing my rich and fruitful life in this book.

CONTENTS

INTRODUCTION

This is the life story of one of the world's greatest hypnotists – Alan Bates. We find him first as a young English schoolboy with just one aim in life – to have as much fun as humanly possible, and at whatever the cost.

You should now be feeling the overwhelming desire to join Alan on his crazy adventure as he takes you through his tough yet crucially formative childhood. "Bates you are going nowhere in life!" (Head Teacher). Just how wrong can you be!

From virtually no qualifications and no future to discovering his talents as an entertainer, we watch as Alan's life takes an upward trajectory that takes him around the world – dining with royalty, ambassadors and high commissioners, even afternoon tea with the President of Malta – onwards and upwards to the very top of his profession.

He's been a toolmaker, disc jockey and broadcaster, cruised the Caribbean as ship's casino manager – but meeting the rich and famous and enjoying the finer things in life paled on discovery of his true talent and vocation, the art of hypnosis.

Skills were honed entertaining in tough back-street clubs before promotion to the giddy heights of theatre, television and, the ultimate pinnacle, the honour of royal performance. He had made it and had become one of the world's greatest hypnotists.

Read also about the life changing potential of hypnotherapy and the countless individuals whose lives have been improved and even saved thanks to Alan's skills. And discover the ghostly and psychic side of life (and death). Journey back in time via tales of strange past life regressions. Hear also Alan's disturbing first-hand accounts of exorcism, haunted houses, and a close encounter with a UFO.

Most of all, this book will leave you feeling positive about life and reassure you that dreams can come true!

Guaranteed to have you spellbound, "ALAN BATES - WIDE AWAKE" is a superb true life story and a compelling read.

CHAPTER ONE
THE EARLY YEARS

Navigating the maze of this world's unpredictability, and guided by the laws of chaos, life can be unfortunate for some and a rich blessing for others. Thankfully, I fall into the latter category; with all the trials and tribulations, good and bad, happy and sad times, overall, my glass has always been half full and never half empty.

To get to know the character of a person through reading a book, I believe it is important to know the background and the early development of the author, so please bear with me as, in this chapter, I build you into my mind-set during the early years.

For my Mum, Joyce Bates, 5th October, 1957, was a very special day, for the first of her three children was born. Times were hard, twelve years after the Second World War the country was still recovering, but life went on, and so, at 3.15 a.m., Alan Bates entered the world in what can be described as rather a quick birth at Highfield Maternity Hospital, Mill Lane, Wallasey, Cheshire. Mum's best friend Doris Henri was Godmother.

I was always going to be a hyperactive child and consequently wore my parents out, and as I grew older my energy increased in abundance, and even now I still possess surprising stamina. And, of course, I personally believe this to be a good thing, as I feel I tend to run rings around most people and get things done.

During this period we lived in a relatively large semi-detached house in Eaton Avenue, Wallasey. We left shortly after to live with my grandparents, John Joseph and Elizabeth Bates – and their pack of dogs – at Tarran Way, Moreton, sharing their home for about two years, and even now I can remember many happy times. The house was a 'prefab', factory-made after the war on a prefabricated design. They were meant only to be a temporary measure, however they lasted a lot longer than intended, and when they were eventually demolished I had an interesting role, which is covered later in this chapter.

We were still living in Wallasey when Mother became pregnant again, and thirteen months after my arrival, Gary Frank entered the world on the 2nd November, 1958.

My Dad, Cyril John, was an engineer employed by the Mersey Docks and Harbour Company, and sailed on the famous Mersey Ferry Boats, working in the engine room transporting passengers to and from Liverpool. He had been a deep sea fisherman when he left school at fourteen, working in horrendous weather conditions, and then had worked shipping our military forces around the world during the Korean conflict, sailing with the merchant navy.

Dad continued to work in his own business up until October 2001 but retired due to ill health. Times were a lot harder then than they are today. Today we live in an increasingly competitive unstable world, where most people in the United Kingdom are better provided for, and generally life has become easier with better conditions, but in my view whether we have better moral values is very questionable.

Mum had left her work before I was born. She had worked for the world-renowned Lever Brothers in Port Sunlight, as a fully trained shorthand typist. When I was seven, Mum eventually went back to work for a legal office in Castle Street, Liverpool. Gary took his middle name from our mother's father, Frank Maldon. He was a coach driver but had tragically died through thrombosis, at just forty-four before Gary was born. At least there is some comfort to know I did get some time with him as a baby. His passing caused great sadness and distress in our family for a very long time, and my poor dear Nan, Mum and her sister Auntie Patricia struggled to cope with the bereavement.

It must have been difficult living with in-laws and bringing up two babies, so when the opportunity arose to have our own home, my parents were delighted. The new home was in Town Meadow Lane, Moreton, Wallasey, where we were to spend many very happy years. The development comprised of several homes or flats, each situated above a row of shops. The area was nicknamed "the Newies" from their completion, but this nickname didn't save them and sadly they in turn were demolished in 2013 to make way for yet another new generation of buildings.

As Gary and I grew through our infancy, we became really close, and this brotherly love has continued. The years passed by and it was time to go to school. We were fortunate that our primary and secondary school were within walking distance. We both attended Lingham junior and middle school in Town Meadow Lane but in a separate year.

The author, aged 3 (1960)

I can still remember my first day at junior school at the ripe age of five. My teacher was named Mrs Platt and I still have the good memories of this kind and gentle lady. Upon recent enquiries, she is still alive and living locally. I was nervous of school at first, as I am sure all the children were on our first day, but we all soon settled in and friendships developed. I was placed at my desk next to a boy called Paul Fell. We became instant good friends and from that day onwards we remained so as we sat next to each other in virtually every class in every school until we left in our sixteenth year. We played together every break-time, and we even sat next to each other every day for school dinner – true friendship.

On our final day at Henry Meols Senior Comprehensive (formerly, Wallasey Grammar School) after we had said our goodbyes to everybody, we walked out the front gate together, removed our school blazers with crested motto and performed the necessary ritual of tearing them up into shreds and discarding them. Occasionally, though, I still reminisce about my school days and I will always hold on to those fond quality memories.

It was in my primary school that I discovered girls. I must have been about six when I found that I liked a girl in my class named Gaynor Roberts. She lived in the road at the back of the school and must have liked me for, as six year olds, we were dared to kiss by the other children. I finally got up the courage after much teasing, went over to her, kissed her so quick on her cheek and ran off as fast as I could. This was my first encounter with girls but my last encounter with Gaynor Roberts. Many friendships were to develop from Lingham junior school and carried right through until we finally moved away to a new area on leaving school at sixteen.

I was very fond of, and close to, my Nan. Nan had married Bill Gannon after Grandad Frank's sudden early death. Bill owned Gannon's removals so there were always lots going on to entertain a young Alan. Nan had a beautiful but boisterous Labrador dog called Jason. He would sometimes go missing for days and then suddenly turn up rotten, dirty and hungry. I used to incorporate Jason in all my games and activities and he would gladly participate in everything. It was during this time that I found my love and respect for all animals, especially dogs. It is my belief that all living things have a fundamental right to live as equally as we humans, no matter how big or small. This ideology I have taught my children, but we are at odds when it concerns wasps and mosquitoes!

I used to love spending time with Nan. She was such a kind, happy and lovely lady, and she used to make the best ever strawberry jam toast and hot tea. In the school holidays I used to help with the removals. It was exciting as a kid to be able to ride in the big wagons and help moving furniture about, and very often I used to get tips off the customers, and Nan paid me wages, too!

As a child and adventurer I was naturally interested in secret passages and hidden tunnels, and one day whilst out on a removal I met Mr. Algernon Plantagenet De-Brotherton. He was a descendant of the royal Plantagenets and was an eccentric old man with a long silvery beard. He lived on the farm where the Upton motorway junction now meets Moreton Road, and due to the local authority acquiring the land with a compulsory purchase order, he had to vacate his home, and subsequently the farm was demolished. While Gannon's men removed his furniture, I chatted with him about his spooky farm house and he showed me a secret tunnel, which apparently led from the farmhouse up to Church Farm on Bidston Hill, and perhaps even beyond. He said that during the war, and on one particular night of heavy German bombing, he entered the tunnel and walked for quite a distance, but part of the tunnel had collapsed and he could continue no more.

I found his story really fascinating but when I told Dad later that evening he had different and not so fond memories of Mr. Algernon Plantagenet De-Brotherton. When Dad was a teenager he used to travel with his friends to the farm and would often take an apple out of his orchard. One day De-Brotherton found them on his land, chased them, and then he opened fire with his shotgun!

Nan secured for me my first Saturday job working for an old grocer near Moreton. He turned out to be one of the meanest people I ever met. As well as trading in the shop, he had an old Commer van, packed to the ceiling with stock, and he used to deliver provisions to local people at their home. My job was to run up and down the stairs as fast as I could, delivering everything from vegetables to soap. One day I was running as fast as I could holding five bottles of lemonade, and of course I tripped and dropped one of them. I had said to him that I couldn't manage that many. I cleaned up, made everything tidy again and continued my work, and then found at the end of the day the mean old sod had deducted the price of the bottle out of my wages. I left this Saturday job after this incident and years later while walking past his premises I was surprised to see the police surrounding his shop – he had been broken into. I remember thinking even at that young age, and maybe wrongfully or maybe over-simplifying it, that karma has perhaps played its part, and that mean people attract other very mean people towards them!

Life around the Newies was a big adventure for most of the children. Not all of our antics are suitable for publishing! However, one of our favourite games at the time was to play bus hopping. The concept was to wait for the local bus to stop to pick up or drop off passengers, and as the driver was preoccupied we would climb and hang on the engine housing at the rear end of the bus and complete the circuit back to where we started. This was really good fun but very dangerous, if our parents knew what we were doing they would have been mortified and we would have been grounded for sure.

We invented a new game and named it "piggy sticks". We would travel to the local brickworks where we knew we could get a good supply of quality clay. We then dug down deep and collected a bag each. Next we searched in the woods to find a tree branch that was very flexible and about two feet long. We then stripped back the bark and this was our new secret weapon; the "piggy stick".

We would now get a handful of our fine clay and mould it around the end of the piggy stick, about four inches from the end. The piggy was now armed and ready. By extending the arm back over the right shoulder and whipping it fast forward the clay would fly off the stick at great speed and after practise was formidably accurate. I will leave the outcome to your imagination...

Time passed and in due course we moved from junior school to middle school. The one subject I excelled at was reading. I loved it. I can remember reading and enjoying book after book. I actually read the whole collection of Enid Blighton's Famous Five, every sentence. These were great adventure books for children and I remember particularly reading one of them where "the Five" had been locked away and one said, "We have been here for so long now that for all we know there could be men on the moon." This was a really interesting coincidence as, while reading this book, on July 20, 1969, Apollo 11 was the spaceflight that landed the first humans on the moon, Americans Neil Armstrong and "Buzz" Aldrin. Amazingly, Armstrong became the first human being to step onto the lunar surface only six hours later.

It is interesting what clear memories we can recall from our past. One particular Sunday, just after Christmas, Gary and I decided to fish the River Mersey off Egremont in Wallasey. It was absolutely freezing cold, snowing, and the visibility was very poor. The boats using the river were sounding their fog horns, a wonderfully romantic "old Liverpool" sound. Along with our friends, Martin and Wayne, we cast out our lines into the River Mersey, drank the hot coffee out of our thermos flasks and jumped up and down to keep warm.

Wayne had a brand new fishing rod and reel for Christmas and was using it for the first time when he stood back and cast his line hard into the icy river. What happened next was disastrous. The bailing arm on the reel jammed and the whiplash pulled the fishing rod right out of his hand and into the water below. Wayne burst into tears as his brother Martin called him every swear word then known to us innocent young boys, and he was ordered by Martin to undress to his underpants, put a life-saving ring around himself, enter the dangerously freezing water and float out to try to rescue his Christmas present – with his feet! The thought of going home without the rod was unimaginable.

At the same time, looking back, the consequences are horribly imaginable as to what could have very easily happened. The end result of this ridiculous action could have been fatal. The River Mersey has taken away many lives in relatively mild conditions never mind the extreme conditions of that day. Surprisingly (!) Wayne could not find the rod with his frozen feet as he was way out of his depth, perishing with cold, and cried his eyes out until we pulled him out of the water. He stood quivering and shaking with hypothermia and we could not even give him a hot drink as we had emptied all our thermos flasks earlier due to the terrible conditions. We continued to fish and shared our rods with Wayne until the tide receded and then we all entered on to the beach in search of the rod. Fortune was with us the rod had not been taken out to sea with the tide and lay semi-submerged in the sand, and Wayne and the rod survived to live and fish another day.

Some of our school holidays were spent under the supervision of Grandad John Joseph Bates, or "Joe" as family and friends called him. My memories of him were good as he was a very gentle and quiet man who had previously before his retirement maintained a hard working life as most people seemed to in pre and post-war Britain. While Mum, Dad and Gran were working, Grandad was left in charge. This was a great time as all Grandad wanted was to sit in his armchair and read book after book and let Gary and I do absolutely anything we wanted to do. Like so many Merseysiders, and my own father, he had been a seafarer, an ex-Royal Navy man, and had travelled the world and worked on mine sweepers during the Second World War. There are rumours that he was torpedoed in the Atlantic Ocean but not unlike a lot of ex-servicemen he did not like to talk about his experiences. At lunchtime he would regularly disappear down to the local pub for a pint of ale. He would then come back home and have an afternoon sleep in his cosy armchair. One particular memory was on the 20th July, 1962, when Grandad took me to Moreton beach to witness the world's first commercial hovercraft arrive. It was a grand affair. There were plenty of press, TV cameras, sightseers and lots of noise. The itinerary was Moreton to Rhyl in North Wales. But, unfortunately for the Wirral, it would never prove to be commercially viable.

Adjacent to our grandparents' home was a large wooded area called Burdens Field. This was named after a big house, long demolished, and which proved a magical adventure land for Gary and me. One cold winter's day we were out playing with our "winter warmers" on Burdens Field. "Winter warmers" were discarded empty tin paint cans which we punched holes in the sides with nails to ventilate the air. A length of copper wire was attached to the tin to act as a handle. We placed bits of paper, twigs and coal, which we dug up from the coal cellar of the old demolished Burdens house, and set alight to the paper. When the fire was under way we swung the winter warmers centrifugally as fast as we could until the coals were ablaze. We would now be able to keep our hands warm as we played in the woods.

How times have changed. Nowadays, children spend so much time in their bedroom on computer games and have no idea how much enjoyment they could have playing outside. We were having a lot of fun climbing trees until a local bully appeared on the scene and demanded he confiscate our fully charged "winter warmers" when Gary, two years the bully's junior, punched him and knocked him to the ground. From that day we never again had a problem with this chap! I can't condone violence, but a valuable lesson was learned that day, it taught me never to intimidate any other person as the experience of being on the receiving end of aggression is psychologically very intimidating. It was unknown to me at this time but I was to save future friends at the hands of a verbal bully by taking exactly the same action as Gary had, and it similarly generated a great feeling of justice.

Mickey Ricketer was an early inspiration to me. He was a tall blond boy one year older than I and a really nice lad. Mickey always had a smile on his face and it was his interest in tinkering with old motorbikes that inspired my interest in engineering. Micky used to roam around the scrap yards looking for interesting things that had been discarded, and one day he found on old moped. He took it home, fixed it, and we used to drive it up and down the beach from Moreton to Meols near Hoylake. I used to ride on the back and for a young boy the excitement of riding fast was such a great thrill. I used to spend my pocket money on petrol, unknown to my mother; she thought I was buying sweets. I was with Micky at the scrapyard when I found an old Villiers 198cc motorbike. My eyes lit up like Christmas tree lights when Mickey said, "Why don't you take it home and try to get it going?" That was it, I needed no more encouragement. Without even thinking what my parents would say I pulled it out of the junk and wheeled it home.

Upon arriving home at the Newies I parked the bike and went to get the garage key. I had to do it sneakily without causing

Boyhood adventurousness continued into adulthood

suspicion. I succeeded and parked the Villiers and went in for dinner. I was that excited I could hardly eat anything; all I wanted was to go back and tinker with the engine. When dinner was over our parents let us play out until it started to go dark. It was a lot safer in these early days because Mum knew we were okay – or so she thought. So off I went to work on my project.

The Villiers was a good old vintage British motorbike. Mine was well rusted but all intact with the exception of the petrol tank, the exhaust pipe and seat. The tank was completely rusted away and there was no way it would contain petrol. As a child I did not have a clue as to where I could get a matching replacement tank so I improvised by using an empty plastic bottle tied to the frame with a piece of string. Once I had solved this problem I filled the bottle with petrol and primed the carburettor using the "tickler". Now was the big moment that I had waited for, is she going to start? I had the bike on its stand and, using the kick-starter, I kicked it over, but sadly there was not even a splutter. I didn't have a clue what to do next. The only thing l could do was to experiment by taking the engine apart. This action I believe was fundamental to my early understanding of things mechanical which had played a big part in deciding which trade to apply for upon leaving school at the age of sixteen. It took quite a while to get the bike to work.

After consulting with friends Mickey, Sam Peeps and Mike Platt, I found the problem to be the electrical points which were seized together. These points act as a switch to supply a current to the spark plug at the correct time in the cycle to ignite the mixture of petrol and air. I took them apart, cleaned and replaced them and asked my friends to push me around the lock-up garages at the back of the Newies – and "bang", she fired once, then a second bang, and, to my amazement, away she went with a huge roar.

As a spectator it must have looked quite a sight to see a little boy balancing on this big motorbike. Unfortunately, due to the exhaust having rusted away in sections, the baffles inside were rattling around and the noise was pretty loud which aroused the curious attention of several local people including my parents! "Alan, get in now!" Mum screamed. "You are grounded and you are not to go near that machine again." The bike was wheeled back to where it was to stay until Mum and Dad had decided its fate. I was still elated due to finally getting the bike to work so my scolding had not even sunk in, going straight over the top of my head. Over the next few days the bike had to stay put. I dared not even wheel it out of the garage. After the heat had subsided a plan was made in school to take the Villiers out for a spin on the "Queen's highway". The plan entailed quietly wheeling the bike past the rear lock-up garages on to a local road. We then primed the machine, put it in gear with the clutch held, pushed until we got a fair speed up, let out the clutch – and she was off. Geoff Platt, a school friend, managed to jump on the back just in time as we sped off down the highway, and I needed to keep the bike running to maintain my balance. Geoff held my waist tight as we powered away. The Villiers was so much more powerful than the moped on which I was used to being a pillion passenger and the excitement was tremendous.

On our second circuit of Wastdale Drive, to my dismay, we passed a police patrol car. I took evasive action and headed quickly back past the lock-ups and through the side entry to our garage with the police car in hot pursuit. I had just enough time to lock up the bike and to make pace into our house. Geoff took off pretty quickly and was away free. Unfortunately for me the police officer must have seen me arriving home and followed me. I went into the house and ran straight up to my bedroom to hide under my bed. Mum answered the door to this big burly policeman and on questioning mum about what he had witnessed he demanded to inspect the motorbike. Upon inspection he was impressed with what he saw – the plastic bottle acting as petrol tank – and due to the fact that I was "only eight years of age!" "...providing the machine was disposed of..." and that I was to be disciplined by my parents, then nothing more was to be said about the matter.

Upon leaving, the officer commented that I was a "clever lad". This was the end of the matter and it was time to say goodbye to my first of many motorbikes, and it would soon be time to say goodbye to Micky as, before long, in the name of progress, the whole of Tarran Way would be demolished to make way for business development.

The fifth of November is a traditional day in Great Britain to celebrate the infamous Guy Fawkes' failed attempt to blow up the Houses of Parliament in 1605. Every town and village throughout the country every year have bonfires and public firework displays, and history informs us that a member of the conspirators involved with the "gunpowder plot" was a man with the surname Bates. I do not know whether he was a family ancestor, but one particular Guy Fawkes evening made a lasting impression on me. The fireworks in my youth were many times more powerful than the ones of present day. Today, "health & safety" have a strict law in place to limit the amount of gunpowder that can be used in the manufacture of fireworks and each year after the big event the statistics and fatalities are reported in the national media.

With the lead up to Bonfire Night, Gary and I, accompanied by Alan Knott, Graham Logan and other friends, were playing at the rear of the Newies, when one of the bigger boys placed a high power Cannon Banger firework in my back pocket with a lit fuse. I realized that something was very wrong and when I tried to remove the banger from my pocket, the burning fuse burnt my fingers and I just couldn't remove it in time, too late, "bang"

– it blew my trouser pocket completely off and left a massive burn and a bruise on my rear end. The pain was terrible and I was rushed home crying and in a distressed state. When my parents heard what happened they went on the warpath to find the culprit. It did not take them long to locate the perpetrator and my parents went round to the boy's home and made their feelings known! That was the end of the matter and I was grateful that I still had my backside intact, several kids that year lost parts of their limbs due to accidents and misuse of the powerful fireworks.

Leasowe lighthouse was a derelict, impressive local landmark situated ten minutes away, built in 1763. It is a fascinating building erected on the Moreton coastline with an internal cast iron spiral staircase rising a hundred feet or more, a focal point for miles around. My local area is steeped in history and has many stories to tell but I don't have the time to tell them here. The Romans had set up a docking station circa 70 AD at Dove Point, a few miles west of our location, in a natural deep-water cove, and they used this base to navigate the River Dee to the ancient city of Chester.

After the Romans came the smugglers. Their tactics included setting fires on our local beach to falsely lure the trading ships away from the River Mersey, whose final trading destination was Liverpool, to run to ground at Moreton. The crew were either murdered or, if lucky, escaped, and the contraband goods taken to hideouts, including that of the famous Old Mother Redcap's cottage in Wallasey, to be sold on the black market. Sometimes when we fished the River Mersey at Wallasey we would often search the grounds of the smuggler's cottage, looking for hidden treasure and the legendary secret passages. Sadly we never found them and the historic cottage, built in 1595, no longer exists. A modern "development" now stands on its ground.

An interesting point to note here is that the Captain of the disastrous Titanic lived only a few miles away from the lighthouse, and I will be telling a ghost story about the Titanic and a close encounter with a UFO at the lighthouse in a later chapter. The base walls of Leasowe lighthouse are about five feet thick and the foundation, as legend has it, is built on the sunken remains of a cotton ship. Every so often adventurers would remove several bricks out of the secured lower window and gain access via a rope, and one afternoon after school in late autumn, just as light was fading, accompanied by several friends we went to the beach and drew straws as to who would be the first to enter this spooky lighthouse. Hearts pounding, once we were all inside we made our way in close line formation with only one torch between us, up the creaky spiral staircase, passing several dark empty rooms on the way, until we reached the top light room. We climbed out on to the small balcony to admire the fantastic views right across the Wirral peninsula, just as the sun finally set in the west over north Wales, and to the north we could see Liverpool and far beyond.

On our dark descent we all congregated in the base room by the entry window, where it was a free for all to get out of the dark scary room while our imaginations played havoc, thinking of the ghosts of a long time past. Looking back it would have looked comical to watch a gang of terrified kids trying all at once to scramble out of one small window. I am very happy to report now that a local trust, The Friends of Leasowe Lighthouse, have taken over the maintenance of this beautiful local treasure, and open days are regular. I have taken my young children on a historic tour, but I am pleased to say that this time the entrance is more civilised – we used the front door!

News was sadly received that the whole of Tarran Way and our early home was to be finally demolished but, of course, there was more fun to be had during the demolition. Adjacent to the brickworks was a very deep water pit. The water was stagnant, slimy, bright green and inhabited by rats and other vermin. All types of rubbish was deposited, from old motorcars to dead cats!

One day my friends Ian Mason, Martin Giles and myself decided to make raft boats out of the old interior and exterior wooden doors from the demolished bungalows. We transported several across to make a raft each and placed them one on top of the other unsecured, until we had about six doors stacked high.

We then launched them out on to the water pit, each of us armed with a length of decorative wooden skirting board to be used as an oar. We paddled out to the centre of the stinking slimy pit, our boats quite stable at this stage, having a lot of fun singing "A Life on the Ocean Wave", until Ian Mason's doors started sliding out from under him. He was buoyant with five doors and then four and then three, but when he went down to two doors the raft became distinctly unseaworthy and he had to abandon ship and jump on to my raft.

I had no say in the matter, he was sinking and his self-preservation kicked in. At first we wobbled a bit, then our raft seemed stable, until the same nightmare scenario started again and my bottom door floated out in front of us. Martin paddled cautiously around, slowly watching the calamity. The next door floated out to the rear, then another. The raft with two people on was now quickly becoming a submarine, and we both looked at Martin, he had weighed up the situation and said quite calmly, "You can sod off. You are not getting on my raft." The situation was now pretty desperate; we sank into the abyss, smelling, swallowing and of course tasting the rotten water as we cried out for help. It was impossible to swim in this mire fully clothed. Martin quickly paddled to shore to raise the alarm as Ian and I remained afloat, holding buoyant pieces of discarded timber and debris, scared to death – literally – I can remember to this day shouting for my Mum.

It was a very dangerous situation we were in. However, Martin was quickly successful in his endeavours and duly returned with a brickworks employee armed with a long length of rubber hosepipe. After several attempts we managed to grasp hold of the pipe and he then dragged us both to safety.

This crazy incident could have so easily gone terribly wrong with tragic consequences had we not been rescued as a real matter of urgency. We were in a state of shock when the employee from the brickworks invited us into the clay kilns to dry out our clothes. We were soaking wet when we walked into the red-hot fired kilns, but within ten minutes we were completely dry and ready to make our way home, a little smelly, to Mum who, upon our arrival, had absolutely no idea of our disastrous day and remained "none-the-wiser". How could I have told her how stupid we were? This was one of the first times that I had thought that it was not my time to meet the Great Architect. But I hadn't completely learnt my lesson and so there were several more very close shaves to come!

Before long my Nan's husband, Bill Gannon, passed away, and on the 28th July, 1971, my dear old Grandad John "Joe" Bates also departed this earth. He was aged 70 and cancer was the cause of his death. This now meant that Nan and Gran were on their own. Granddad's funeral was held at the church in Moreton Cross and it was the first burial / funeral I ever attended. It left an indelible impression on my mind and I firmly believe that young children should be sheltered from funerals unless it is totally necessary. Grandad was buried at Frankby Cemetery, Wirral.

I get a wonderful feeling of nostalgia each time I travel to this part of Moreton and the long distant happy childhood memories of the care free times are still prevalent. I would not change any part of this period in my life for anything. In October 1971, our parents had the opportunity to move home. A nice cottage came on the market and before long we were to move, leaving behind the joyful playground of Town Meadow Lane. The next stage in my life was about to unfold.

CHAPTER TWO
MIND SET

By now a profile is probably emerging in your mind, and, I hope, you have more understanding of my character and mindset. Partly set by history, driven by the times and the conditions we lived through. And also partly psychological perhaps, forming from my particular responses to those restrictions and opportunities presented to us in the Britain of the late fifties and sixties, as was related in the previous chapter.

Now, I am not hypnotising you, yet, I hope. I am merely showing how my die was cast, before I guide you into my professional life. There are some more formative times, two more schools, a college apprenticeship and employment on several cruise ships that I would like to share with you. So, if you will, spend a little more time with the younger me, to see those times and that world through my eyes.

For example, education is a very important element in any child's life, and, in most cases – depending on what degree of education you receive – naturally determines the type of employment one eventually seeks. But, I really just don't think this applied in my case! Most of us have some memories of our early education; I certainly do. Let me take you to Moreton Secondary Modern, or M.S.M., my new school.

I don't know where on earth the school sourced the teachers from, but they were a vast array of exceptionally strange and eccentric characters. My maths teacher was a Mr. Alfred Shadrack, "Alfie for short". Let me give you an example. I started on a certain maths page the day I arrived at the school and upon leaving that school I was still on that same page! We received no tutoring in maths and we – particularly me – did nothing but fool around. But, even if we had wanted to study, we would not have stood a chance.

Alfie possessed a large wooden blackboard ruler and if he caught you misbehaving he would put a vote to the whole class as to what punishment the act should merit? The entire class was always, unanimous as to the punishment – punishment by a massive hard strike with the board ruler to the seat of your pants, though with this subtle little difference: he would write in chalk on the board ruler "kcams", so that after the board ruler had hit its target, it would be translated to "smack" on your black school uniform trousers. He also used lots of other different words which reflected his moods of the day, and which of course stayed there on display for some considerable time and for all to see. Can you imagine this happening today?

And yet we all looked forward to lessons with "Alfie", and the highlight of every lesson was cheering very loudly as somebody was chosen to be whacked! Sometimes he would choose the pupil and sometimes he would ask the class to nominate a recipient – even if no misdemeanour had taken place! I was no exception to getting whacked, but craftily I would pad out my trousers with writing paper in advance to soften and cushion the blow.

We had a very strict English teacher named Mr. John Larkin. "Johnny Larkin" was a teacher who did not suffer fools gladly – but we all liked him. If you so much as spoke out of place, he would throw the wooden chalk duster at you with such precision and severe force that it would leave a lump on your head the size of a golf ball. And often he would run down the aisle of pupils and physically throttle the misbehaving student.

In the present day, this behaviour would not be tolerated. But, at the time – and with us kids – it was required and accepted. Looking back, I would have to say that we seemed to need this level and type of discipline to keep us under control. And we completely accepted it. In fact, I used to enjoy English lessons with Johnny Larkin most of all, and he really got through to us.

Considering music was to play a big role financially later in my life, it may be surprising to know that during my school education I had absolutely no interest in the subject – none whatsoever. I can remember quite well attempting to sing in the school choir in Lingham Middle School and the music teacher informing me that I "would not be needed"!

During my "education" at M.S.M., I was seriously glad that my interests did not include music, as the music teacher was very weird. The students had nicknamed him Dudley Moore, or "Dud" for short. We seemed to have nicknames for all of our teachers, the good ones and the bad. Dud was a bad one. He used to prey on the weakest members of each class he took, and he, without fail, would pick on somebody every lesson. Fortunately, he must have seen me as one of the mentally stronger members of the class and he left me alone.

His sick behaviour would start by calling a pupil to come out from his chair. He would direct him into the storeroom annexed to the classroom and stand on the unwilling student's toes so that it was impossible to move or get away. His next procedure was to pull out the boy's shirt and then put his hands into his trousers, while at the same time saying, "Who dressed you this morning? Your shirt's hanging out," as he tucked the shirt back in his trousers. At the same time this was happening, the whole class would sing lines, including, "Dudley's a queer, Dudley's a queer."

On several occasions, parents would come to the school and seriously protest about this behaviour, but he was never fired, nor to my knowledge ever prosecuted or even reprimanded, and he continued in his post throughout my time at the school. So, some things have certainly changed for the better, and this activity would not be allowed nowadays. I hope.

Every end of school term however was "karma time" for Dud's wrong doings. Due to the fact he used the "Mersey line" rail network to travel home, dozens of boys would line up at the station and pelt him with eggs and stones, this practise was a regular ritual. And necessary, too, indeed on one end of school-term during an English lesson with "Johnny Larkin", Johnny stood up and very sternly said, "Now listen to me very clearly. As you know, today is the end of school-term and for those of you who are going to greet "Dudley" at the station, I do not want any of you to throw anything at him – anything, that is, under 'Half Bricks!'"

As you can imagine this statement was greeted with a loud cheer. Johnny finished by saying, and in his words, "Mr Moore is not only a sick swine but he is a very nasty man." I have memories of lining the station platform with the other boys and throwing rotten eggs!

Educational progression, if that is what I can call it, directed me to my final school, the Henry Meols Senior Comprehensive. This was a move up the education ladder as pupils from all over the region attended. There was a better ethos here, and greater opportunity to get a good education at this school, if you cared to study and work hard that is. Now, no one likes to think they are stupid, but situations can sometimes make us feel that way. I was not great at school but because of my previous lack of education I was at a serious disadvantage and needed to go some to catch up with the other pupils.

We new pupils were soon to find our feet and to assess all our teachers. And of course we found them to be all different sorts of characters and types and eventually we, and they, found our limitations, and we tested their patience and skill levels. Knowing just how far we could go was a most important observation, vital, in fact. The only subject I was interested in was the metalwork class and the class master was a Mr. Donald Mackey, "Donny Mac" for short. He was a quality craftsman and I owe a great debt to this man's inspiration. It was in this class that I was to make another long-term good friend, Graham Pitt. Graham was also keenly interested in motorbikes and all things mechanical and we attended the metalwork night-school class once a week all the time we were at school, and, between us both, we won the school prize for engineering every year.

I was starting a sort of family tradition here as my brother Gary followed me into Henry Meols. And then we gained another family member, brother John Maldon Bates. John was born on the 8th January, 1972. John followed in our footsteps at this school and outshone us two when he attained the position of "Head Boy" and received the "Scholar of the year award". John was a real achiever whose hard work and effort led to his receiving personally from HRH Prince Philip, The Duke of Edinburgh, the Duke of Edinburgh's Gold Award!

Achievement, I feel, needs to be measured in terms of the circumstances in which it was won. John, a decade after us, achieved a terrific education and then built on it to gain further excellent results and a degree at Manchester University. Considering my very poor academic attainments, with the notable exception of engineering – which I loved – the headmaster, Mr. Gordon, commented reasonably on completion of my school career, *"Bates you are going nowhere in life."*

I can reflect back to this period and Mr. Gordon certainly did have a very valid point. Fortunately, the Universe had very different plans for me!

For the first time, probably like many youngsters, I was at a complete loss as to what I was going to do with my life. And it really did hit me hard upon leaving school. Engineering had been the only subject I had really enjoyed and excelled at so it seemed like a natural progression when I was drawn in that direction.

I felt truly lost and it dawned on me that now I had to do something about it. So I applied to several engineering companies, but at that time, and probably from that time onwards in the north-west, there were just no jobs available. My parents were concerned, here was their eldest son, able and willing and desperately wanting a job, but with no qualifications other than a distinction in engineering, in an employment area depressingly in decline. It is commonplace now, but back then it was a real shock. In our parents' era there had always been work for skilful people, particularly in the industrial heartland of the north.

Mum made it her remit to try on my behalf by telephoning several companies, and just when she was tiring with all the similar negative responses that I had received, she struck gold with a Mr. Les Cope at Design Tools & Gauges (DT&G) in Wallasey. Mum told him how much I loved engineering and how good I was and that I had also won the school prizes. She turned my luck that day. Mr. Cope informed Mum that the company was indeed looking to take on an apprentice toolmaker/mechanical engineer and that I should attend an interview at the factory at 10.00 a.m. on the following Monday morning. It was a terrific feeling knowing that someone wanted to take me on, I finally had a chance of a job and I knew that it was so important that I do my upmost and not let my mother down.

I arrived early for my interview, punctuality was an essential factor in any interview, and nervously I approached the factory. DT&G were based on the Dock Road in Wallasey and the factory was situated on the first floor. I entered the building and climbed the old Victorian staircase to their main entrance door, but with my head held high I knocked on the door and entered into the factory. I had just enough time to conduct a quick 360 degree scan of the place before I was approached by a gentleman, smartly dressed in a bright white overall, shirt and tie. He gave me a welcoming smile and said, "Good morning you must be Alan Bates". "Yes sir," I replied. "Welcome to Design Tool & Gauges. My name is Les Cope, general manager. Please call me Les."

Straight away I got a good feeling about this man. I felt I could trust him. He could see I was nervous and he tried his best to make me feel welcome and at ease. I was given a guided tour of the factory and Les introduced me to some of the employees, giving a brief explanation on what engineering projects they were working on. I thought the place was fantastic. The factory contained a vast array of lathes, milling machines and cylindrical grinders, and each engineer had his own workbench. I was very impressed and at the end of the interview Les even thanked me for attending and said he would be in contact within the week. I left the factory feeling drained but very, very positive – I still kept my fingers firmly crossed in the hope of having being successful in my first ever interview.

I don't know how many other applications they had but I did not have to wait long for Les to get in touch. The next day he telephoned Mum and informed her that I was successful in my interview and that I was to start work with DT&G on the 17th June, 1974, on a four year apprenticeship with a paid day release each week to attend Wallasey College of Further Education. I was beside myself with genuine excitement. Not many school leavers would be so lucky that year, nor since. I had not just a job, but an *engineering apprenticeship*. And to this day I have Mum and Les Cope to thank for this amazing opportunity.

Now, apprentice pranks are the bane and the spice of engineering life, and duly, during my apprenticeship, I was caught out twice. The first time I fell for the legendary comic mission of being told to go to the jig-boring bay which is a room with a large boring engineering machine, and ask one Peter Craven for "a long stand".

Peter, of course, rudely and completely ignored me while he worked on at some engrossing project. After waiting a further twenty minutes and giving several requests, I asked him again for a long stand and he replied, "Alan surely you have had a long enough one now – LEAVE!"

The second one that was played on me also concerned Peter Craven. Late one Friday afternoon, just before the end of a long working day, Peter was working alone in the same jig-boring basement room. He was face skimming a very large diameter flange when he suffered a terrible accident. The machine was rotating on a low speed and Peter rested his hand in a certain position on the tool mount. With each revolution, Peter would brush off the discarded metal swarf with a small brush at the same time he was reading the newspaper. He became complacent and mistimed the correct brush stroke when the cutting tool ripped two of his fingers clean off just above the knuckle. Peter was rushed to hospital.

In these days of health and safety initiatives, it's sobering to remember just how many serious and debilitating accidents used to happen in the workplace, and the black humour with which we met them.

On the following Monday I was working on a turning lathe when Terry Doyle, another engineer, approached me with a small mysterious box in the palm of his hand. Terry said quietly, in a serious manner while looking over his shoulder, "Alan you will never believe what I have in this box." Hesitantly, I enquired, "What Terry?" "Peter Craven's fingers." "No way" I responded. Slowly, he opened the box, while telling me he had handpicked them out of the discarded swarf waste on the machine. As he carefully opened the box, I gasped at the sight of two macabre, blackened fingers, resting on a white tissue, caked with blood at the severed ends. I was in a state of shock – this was not something that one expects to see first thing on a Monday morning.

"I dare you to touch them," Terry said. I was always up for a dare and without question I reached out to touch them when, to my astonishment, they wiggled in the box. Terry had me completely and I jumped right out of my skin. It took me some time to recover and to realise that Terry had made a hole in the bottom of the box and the fingers were indeed his. It worked perfectly. The "dead" fingers, stained and bloodied, looked *so* real, which of course they were!

Before leaving school I regularly attended a local youth club in Moreton. This was the breeding ground for my later professional involvement in the entertainment and music industry. It was here that I became interested in entertaining people and entrancing them with the music of the day – disco and soul music. I loved playing these genres and watching people dance and be captured by the music.

So I bought a share in a mobile disco and, apart from working the youth club, I was now getting paid to play at private parties, weddings and birthday celebrations, this fascinating occupation now running parallel to my apprenticeship. And there was a case of irony here. I was now earning more money in my DJ career than by engineering. But I was still enjoying the "hands on" making and building aspect of engineering. Both areas tugged at me but entertainment seemed to just tug harder.

And the crossover point between working the private parties, etc., over to working the professional nightclub scene was inevitable. The image of a mobile DJ had to change. The groundwork and DJ training was now complete and I knew in my heart I was ready for the transition. My first nightclub residency was performing weekly at the Odd Spot nightclub in Bold Street, Liverpool. The club had seen better days and was now a rather tired and run down place but it was the "royal road" to many grander clubs that were to come my way. Shortly after I moved on to the seaside town of New Brighton and another club called the Penny Farthing. The nightclub scene was now playing a leading part in my life and my apprenticeship was bound to suffer, due to the late nights and me burning the candle at both ends – and often in the middle, too. But, again, fortunately for me, big changes were in the air.

My four-year apprenticeship with DT&G was now complete and I was now a duly qualified engineer; likewise, I graduated from my college. I received my City & Guilds Certification attaining a distinction in Craft Principals and Applications, Electrical Principals and Applications and passes in General Studies and English. I had proved to my family, Les Cope and most importantly to myself that I could do it. I had come a long way from mischief-making at school with virtually no qualifications – and, let's face it, very few prospects – to a fully time served City & Guilds Engineer!

I had once again come to an important crossroad in my life. I found it difficult and tiring to maintain both occupations. "Luckily" I had made a good friend during my apprenticeship whose name was John Maguire. John operated his electronic company, Liverpool Electronics, within DT&G, and one day I told him my predicament. His reply was direct: "Would you like to go to Miami in the United States and work on a Cruise Ship?" Now, John was a renowned practical joker and often joked with me, but I noted a tone of seriousness in his voice. Before I could reply, I was called away on duty.

The next day when he approached me again and asked whether I had made up my mind about leaving England and going to work on the cruise ships, I realised he was very serious. It turned out that a friend of John's was on a recruitment drive for Carnival Cruise Lines, based in Florida, and he was interviewing at the Moat House Hotel in Liverpool. John said, "If you want the job, Alan, it is yours, but you will have to make up your mind, and pretty quickly."

This proves yet again that it is who you know and not what you know. I had only the one evening to think it over; John needed an answer the very next day. After work, I talked it over with my family and again later in the pub with my close friends. I came to the conclusion that I had to go. It was not an easy decision but I felt I just had to.

I did not know at the time but this was to be one of many big lucky breaks I was to get in life. I was so excited that night I found it difficult to sleep, thinking about how to break the news to Les Cope, putting on hold my DJ career, and saying goodbye to family and friends. Apart from a holiday in the Isle of Man, which is only a short hop from the Wirral, I had not travelled outside of England. This for sure was to be a massive step in my life and a serious change and challenge to my lifestyle. The next day I arrived at work and I gave John my answer. He smiled. I think that he knew this was a good decision and, I believe, secretly, he wanted me to go. He was very good to me.[1]

A big Saturday night leaving party in Liverpool was now duly planned, with all my good friends in attendance. Mark, who was also an engineer, had landed himself a new job in Toronto, Canada, and he was leaving England around the same time as me, so we combined our celebration together. It seemed to make good sense as we mainly shared the same group of friends. The soiree started really well. About twenty friends in high spirits turned out for what was to become a serious drinking binge. Mark had driven over in his car to Liverpool with a very good intention to leave it parked and pick it up the next day after recovering from the party hangover.

The evening went very well. We attended many well-known pubs and a disco at the famous Atlantic Hotel, and, at two in the morning, when the disco ended, it was time to make our way home. By now, most of our friends had dwindled. Some went off with girls they met that night and some just got lost in the drunken mist of the early morning. The remaining guys gathered around a street hot dog seller and plans were made to get home. Mark made a very bad decision to drive his car home. His car was a little Hillman Avenger and there were nine of us. Mark suggested seven in the car and two in the boot. What a wonderful idea!

Due to alcohol and Dutch courage I volunteered, along with another friend, Ronnie, to travel in the boot. Ronnie and I wedged ourselves in the boot first and the rest of the lads squeezed into the rather small family saloon. We could hear the jovial conversation and singing clearly from inside the boot and at the time it seemed perfectly acceptable being locked in the boot of a car with an inebriated driver in the city centre of Liverpool early hours on a Sunday morning. Mark, clearly over the drink drive limit, started the car and proceeded in the general direction of the Mersey Tunnel and home.

Unknown to Mark he was driving down a one-way street the wrong way when we clearly heard from within the boot the siren of a police vehicle getting closer and closer. Ronnie and I could hear all the blasphemy, ribald conversation and siren as the police riot van signalled Mark to stop. Several police officers jumped out and surrounded the car. Mark wound his driver side window down and said in an inebriated manner, "Good efin, osofer, can I help us?" The policeman's first response was, "You have stolen this car, haven't you, lad?" "Abso – absolutely – way, no. Ask me frens." The agitated officer of the law put his head in the window and counted, "One, two, three, four, five, six, and the driver, seven. You are in serious trouble, son. Step out of the vehicle. Now!" The officer's next words were, "And what have you got in the boot of your car son?" Mark replied, "More mates." The *bobby* slapped him hard across the head and demanded he open the boot at once!

The police in Liverpool had a well known reputation of taking no messing around. Ronnie and I could hear the dialogue as Mark did as requested and opened the boot. I sprang out in jovial manner like a coiled spring, to the total shock of the policeman. His immediate response was to apprehend me in a vice-like grip, place handcuffs on my wrists and proceed to frogmarch me into the stationary police vehicle, citing my arrest for being drunk and disorderly. Mark failed a roadside breath test and was immediately arrested and charged with drink driving and driving down a one-way street the wrong way. The rest of the lads had their names and addresses recorded and were then told they were free to leave.

I was escorted to the Cheapside Bridewell police station, officially charged with drunk and disorderly conduct and placed in an old Victorian cell inhabited by four very rough and dirty looking tramps. One young one was covered in blood and I asked him what he had done. He replied that he had got a good beating from the police for punching "a bitch of a policewoman" in the face.

By now I had totally sobered up and I knew definitely that I did not belong in this environment. I had been having a very enjoyable and trouble free evening with good friends. The only reason I was in this situation was because I had startled the police officer when he initially opened the car boot. Ronnie, my companion, had not been arrested and he was also in the boot. An old drunken Irish tramp in the cell was wailing, shouting and banging on the door. "Help me, help me! They are stealing my watch and now they have thrown it out of the window." The poor guy was obviously hallucinating. There was no window in the cell and he didn't own a watch. If he did, it would have been taken at the time he was booked in. The cell was a long, foreboding and ancient brick tunnel-like structure with a cold damp stone floor. There was a dirty "open plan" communal toilet at one end, and several wood benches to lie awake on all night. It was going to be a long, stressful and very uncomfortable night ahead.

Eight o'clock in the morning, the key turned in the lock, followed by a loud banging at the door and a burly police officer, fresh on the Sunday morning shift, shouted my name and bailed me to appear before the city magistrates on the Tuesday morning at 10.00 a.m. Phew! It was a relief to get out of that hellhole. I have great respect for the British police force and some of my good friends are serving police officers. I now had first-hand experience of what they have to deal with on a daily basis and I have to commend them.

It was cutting things very fine. I was due to fly out to Miami on the 18th April. If things went wrong, I could miss my flight and miss the opportunity of a lifetime. Under different circumstances, I would have pleaded not guilty to the charge of drunk and disorderly, as I truly believed I was innocent. Yes, I was drunk, but I was certainly not disorderly. But I was informed if I pleaded guilty, and by virtue of the fact it was my first and only offence, I would receive a small fine and that would be the end of the matter. I was also informed the offence was a civil misdemeanour and not a criminal matter, but if I pleaded not guilty then I would again be bailed for a future court appearance, putting my new job in jeopardy. So, although it went against the grain, I decided to plead guilty.

Tuesday morning arrived and, dressed in my best suit, I duly attended and presented myself to the city magistrate's court. The waiting room contained many undesirables, very rough and unkempt, and I stood out looking more like a trainee solicitor than a defendant! My name was eventually called, along with several other men on similar charges. The defendant before me had no manners, and when asked, "Guilty or not guilty?" he simply replied in a gruff manner, "Guilty." "Do you have anything to say?" asked the Magistrate "No," he replied. He was fined twenty pounds and instructed he had two weeks to pay. The court usher addressed the bench, "Next, your worships, is Mr. Alan Bates," and the charge sheet was read out. "Mr. Bates, how do you plead to this charge?" asked the magistrate. I observed him taking in my smart appearance. "Guilty, sir," I replied. "Before I pass sentence, do you have anything to say?" he asked. "Yes, sir. I would first like to apologise for all the inconvenience that I have caused. It was totally out of my character to behave in such a manner." And then I proceeded to explain my reason for the celebration and the fact that I was leaving England for Florida. The court fell completely silent as everybody listened to my story and, when I finished, the three magistrates put their heads together and quietly discussed my punishment, finally concluding, "Mr. Bates, we find you guilty as charged and the court fines you ten pounds," – ten pounds cheaper than the previous ill-mannered defendant – "but, on behalf of the court, we all wish you well with your career. Good luck and safe travel. I trust you will pay today and you are free to go."

I paid the court clerk my ten pounds out of a large bundle of cash under the watchful eyes of several very rough looking characters. I waited for my receipt, rushed out of the building and ran as fast as I could, not stopping until I reached the underground rail network that would take me under the River Mersey and safely home.

And in just a few hours' time, my life would take a completely different direction and be totally changed forever!

[1] *Many years later, bad news arrived on my doorstep which upset me greatly. John had suffered a massive heart attack while working and had died at the roadside. I attended his funeral. He was a dear friend.*

CHAPTER THREE
CRUISING

Cruising America

After virtually no sleep, watching the hours on my luminous alarm clock tick by, dawn finally broke and the new chapter in my life was about to begin. Packed and ready to go, I said farewell to my parents, brothers Gary and young John, and, with many, many mixed emotions, I set off by train from Liverpool's infamous Lime Street station to London's Heathrow airport. I was to meet up with a fellow Liverpudlian, Alan Williams, who was to be the ship's electronics engineer. Alan proved himself to be a great guy. He was down to earth, intelligent, very funny and, in many ways, an "archetypal" scouser.

After a long eight hour flight, our plane touched down, just after lunch, at Miami International airport. At the airport we found Cliff on time at the pre-arranged meeting point. After a brief conversation we made our way through the arrival doors into the heat and the intense brightness of the Florida day. Cliff suggested a quick visit to downtown Miami for a quick bite to eat and then we were to board our cruise ship, *Carnival,* which was due to sail that night.

I was deeply impressed with Miami. It was a fascinating place to me, so clean and beautiful. Wherever you looked, there were vivid blue skies, waving palm trees and, looking out to sea, a gleaming shimmering ocean. I really thought, any moment, I was going to wake up from a dream, or this movie that apparently I was starring in!

After our brief guided tour we arrived at the harbour and another great sight awaited us – all the brightly coloured cruise ships, neatly lined up, glittering in the afternoon sun. We watched the excited passengers boarding their ships, undoubtedly looking forward to their vacation. We felt exactly the same as we boarded *Carnival* and followed Cliff to the cocktail bar where the Casino staff were chilling out, drinking afternoon iced tea. I actually shivered with excitement thinking I was going to be part of this scene and this new world.

Cliff introduced me to the casino staff and members of the entertainment crew, they were mainly British, with some Americans and a few Puerto Ricans. I found them all to be very friendly. And I also noticed they were as curious of me as I was of them. This was the first time I'd ever been a foreigner anywhere, and it was such a big and very pleasant surprise when you realise that you, too, are every bit as "exotic" and different as these exotic and different folk you are standing and working amongst.

Cliff then took me to my place of work – the casino. The name itself sounded pure James Bond to me. The casino was always closed and secured with a special seal while the ship was in port. Just to open the door would contravene the serious U.S. gambling laws. I had never been inside a casino before. Gambling and betting was in my view (and still is) a mug's game. Hard earned money, I believe, was not to be gambled with, and this was proved to me many times as I watched ordinary people lose lots of money in these casinos.

The uniformed customs officers boarded the ship and removed the door seals and, upon entering for the first time, I was taken aback at the unique atmosphere. The deep rich colours of the gambling tables and the shining chrome of the Bally slot machines stood out to my eyes. Cliff opened up one of the machines and gave me an electrical mechanics quick guided "tour" of its workings. "In no time at all you will be able to fix anything that goes wrong inside this baby." I was frozen to the spot. I thought to myself that I had no chance of doing this. Just the sight of all the cables, circuits and relays! It looked so complicated. I was just about to say I didn't think I could handle this when Cliff came out with, "Right, let's go and get you fitted out for your tuxedo. The casino opens very soon and we start work." I followed Cliff to the fitting room where I was given a very smart, fully fitted tuxedo, frilly shirt and black velvet bowtie.

It was all happening so fast. Within that last twenty-four hours, I had said my first farewell to my family, jetted off to America, toured and dined in downtown Miami, met up with my flamboyant and exotic new friends, been decked out in a really sharp tuxedo – and I was to start work in a casino within the hour!

An announcement was made over the public address system. "Would all none passengers please vacate the ship; the *Carnival* will set sail in five minutes." And true to these words, within minutes we felt the ship moving off. The captain began to address the passengers with a welcome speech and the crew gave the necessary safety instructions. And as soon as the formalities were complete, the casino was declared open and I was at work.

All the casino staff were smartly dressed in eveningwear and stationed at their respective gambling tables. We had several blackjack tables, roulette, a joker seven table and around fifty Bally slot machines. As the casino doors swung open, there was a rush of people – just like Black Friday at Christmas – and all very eager to leave their money with us. I was still jet lagged and tired from my trip and I was given a bunch of keys and Cliff instructed me how to clear a simple coin jam which was the simple most common problem. To my mind this was due totally to the eagerness of the punters not being able to put their money in the machines fast enough!

It was not long before they, and I, realised that I was not just a slot machine technician but also a public relations manager. Whenever a client had a problem they asked for the 'manager', and I was called to help and assist them and as soon as I spoke a word with my English accent I was immediately the centre of attention, they wanted to know all about me and where about in England I came from and whether I knew the Beatles! This question was asked so many times I soon began to use it as a chat up line. Eventually it grew worse until Paul McCartney became a regular guest at my parents for traditional Sunday lunch. It worked very successfully. But I didn't mention any of it when I did get to meet Paul many years later while learning to fly at Liverpool airport.

That first night passed very smoothly and when I finally fell into my cabin in the early hours I was asleep before my head touched the pillow.

I was woken early the next morning by my room maid. So every aspect of my new life was going to be very different and it hadn't melted away overnight. There were going to be so many different ways of doing things and so much to learn. I showered and went to breakfast in one of the restaurants. The *Carnival* was a nice old ship but took a lot of getting used to. There were several large dining rooms, lots of small bars, larger lounges, a discotheque, cinema, several swimming pools, shops, a hospital, and seemingly dozens of passenger decks with hundreds of corridors. It was very easy to get lost and I did lots of times as they all looked the same, but before long I had it all mastered. And, also, it has to be said, I often found myself being walked to strange cabins slightly drunk and had to find my way back later on when I was sober.

The mornings were spent working; firstly, on the slot machines that had broken down the previous night. If the machine could not be fixed within ten minutes we closed it off until there was more time, perhaps the next day. Then, on to servicing, and preventive maintenance was also carried out during the rest of the morning. We would normally have completed our tasks by lunchtime and the rest of the day would be our own.

I was settling in nicely making new friends all the time including the seamen and stewards on board the ship. The nationalities were various – West Indians, South Americans and Europeans, and I was known as "Rubio" (meaning Blondie) by the South Americans. The ship's officers were generally unkind to the staff that carried out the menial and necessary everyday tasks, but I always had time for them and, in fact, this was the way I picked up bits of the Spanish language. I learned an important lesson on the *Carnival* and that lesson was to always treat people the way you would like to be treated. And, do you know, it works really well. I was making some fascinating friends and met some great characters including the cousin of the famous Bob Marley and his band, The Wailers, from Jamaica; his name

The casino, and a bad hair day

was Charles Darwin (no relation to the other Charles Darwin). During an uprising in Kingston, Charles had been shot in the face. Miraculously, the bullet passed straight through his fleshy cheek, missing his teeth and a vital artery, and came out at the back of his neck, resulting in only a small scar on his face but a messy wound at the back of his neck.

One night I was invited by Charles to a party below decks, so when I finished my work Charles came to meet me and escorted me into the depths of the ship that I had never explored. The music got louder and louder as we approached the party and when the door opened there must have been fifty West Indian guys, all dancing to serious reggae music, and I was the only white face at the party. I was made very welcome, and as the guys

45

knew I was a DJ back in England, escorted over to the sound system where I was given the job of playing whatever I wanted. As fast as I could drink a beer, there was another guy waiting on me with another. The next day, I thanked Charles again for the party invitation and asked him what the celebration was for. He replied, "Jamaica Independence Day from the British"!

I truly loved every day of my new life. I suppose that I was still finding my feet during the first couple of weeks but time just flew and all the jobs were becoming easier. I started trying new types of food, from flying fish to lobster, filet mignon steaks to flambé ice cream, first class wines and champagnes from all over the world, all while meeting very interesting people, mainly from the States. I had also mastered the electrical mechanics of the Bally slots and was slowly getting more confident with them, able to sort out most of their problems. I even started seeing jackpots in my sleep.

Alan Williams and I decided to take a scuba diving course in St. Thomas, the American Virgin Island. We sourced a reputable PADI registered dive school and enrolled on their course. The course was over a six-week period, one full day per week, and our instructor, George Kremer, was an American dive master. The clear warm beautiful water of Cokey Point proved a terrific place to learn to dive. Over the weeks we were instructed on all aspects of diving and emergency procedures and eventually took our main diving test, which we both passed with flying colours on the 4th July, 1978. We were then issued with our two licences, the PADI and the *Brevet International de Plongee Sous-Marine* premier star degree. Shortly after, we bought all our own equipment and went out on our own dives.

Carnival's weekly cruise itinerary comprised Miami for one day, disembarking and embarking passengers, followed by one full day and night at sea, then on to Freeport in the Virgin Islands, St. Martin, St. Lucia, St. Thomas, Puerto Rico and back to Miami. Several months had passed when one day Cliff came to see me and said, "Change of scenery for you, Alan. You are to change ship and run your own casino on *Carnival's* sister ship,

46

the *Mardi Gras*." It was quite a shock. I had settled in nicely and was enjoying myself immensely on the *Carnival* but I accepted the move and took it as a compliment – Cliff trusted my ability to manage the Casino.

Arrangements had been made for croupiers Willy Betancourt, José, Barbara and myself to disembark at St. Martin and wait a few days to pick up our new ship to cruise over to the Panama Canal and the final destination, Long Beach, California. I decided to take the opportunity to get a suntan but was warned by Willy to be very careful with the sun's rays. So, of course, I ignored Willy's warning and for the whole of the first day I sunbathed by the hotel pool in one hundred and ten degrees heat with no sun protection whatsoever. Late afternoon, I went for a walk around the local shops when a native of St. Martin stopped me in the street and ordered me to cover up or face severe sun stroke. I told him I was fine and he walked off shaking his head. He was right and so was Willy – early evening, I started feeling ill and retired to my hotel room to sleep. I was severely sunburnt and very dehydrated and when Willy came to visit me he suggested I go to hospital. But I was so embarrassed I just put on a brave face – a very red brave face – and I declined his suggestion.

Willy and the others were all going out for dinner and suggested I use room service and arrangements were made to meet the following day. I fell asleep for a few hours and when I awoke I was hallucinating. I could hear a lot of commotion, flashing blue and red lights and people banging and shouting at my door. I went back to sleep and when I awoke in the morning I felt slightly better and my head had stopped spinning. My skin had blistered all over and it was very difficult to even move but I dressed and made my way to the reception. On the way through the corridor I smelt a very strange smell of burning but, thank god, it wasn't my skin. To my horror, when I reached the reception, or what was left of the reception, I was informed by a porter that during the night the hotel had had a fire and a large section had completely burnt down. The noises I could hear, the banging on the doors during my hallucination, was a genuine alarm to vacate the hotel. I was so close to meeting my maker but again it just was not my time!

I joined my new ship, the *Mardi Gras,* which was very similar in design to the *Carnival. E*ventually, I was introduced to all my new casino colleagues. I was still really unwell, my skin rustled when I walked. And it was nearly one week before I was fit to do any work whatsoever. I was very, very embarrassed at what I had done. But I had learned a very valuable lesson – never to underestimate the power of that sun. At those latitudes, it can be lethal. It took time but my body recovered and I started to feel much better. Soon I got to know all the casino staff who were mainly Hispanic and usually kept themselves to themselves. They were nice people but not as adventurous and outgoing as their British and American colleagues.

This one-off cruise proved very interesting as it took me to destinations I had never dreamed about, including Curacao, Cartagena, Puerto Vallarta, Acapulco and, our final destination, Long Beach, California. I remember being really impressed by Acapulco. We were warned to be careful at night as muggings were common down there, but I thought I was pretty streetwise and never worried about the dangers. It certainly didn't stop me from visiting the bars and clubs. I learned to water-ski in the beautiful warm water and I also tried parascending, which I thought was exhilarating. Diane, an American pal from the ship, tried it after me but she was very unlucky. As the powerboat took up the slack in the rope and the boat applied power she tripped and was dragged over the beach and the rocks before she eventually became airborne. After her session was over and she was dropped onto the beach crying and in a dreadful state, we went over to her and covered her up as her swimsuit had been torn off. After consoling her, it wasn't long before her good spirits returned and in no time at all we were having a good laugh about the whole incident over several cold beers. We worked out that I had spent my entire week's salary in just over 24 hours! I had a marvellous time and I enjoyed spending my very last dollar.

The Panama crossing was very interesting. The ships were stacked in a long queue, all waiting in turn for their time slot to enter the canal. Due to the long wait, we decided to hold a party. After which, I have to admit, I retired about four in the morning very inebriated. I was woken up that morning by housekeeping trying to push open the door past a heavy obstacle. That obstacle was me. Luckily, I made it just in time to witness the crossing; we had entered the locks as I surfaced on deck and the captain gave the passengers and crew a superb running commentary of the whole process via the ship's intercom.

California is a wonderful place. We had two days to play before we headed back to the Caribbean and went shopping and sightseeing. And it was here that I witnessed a chap getting a ticket from the police for "jaywalking". As a Brit I thought, what a cheek fining somebody for just crossing the flaming road! We had lunch aboard the famous British museum ship the *Queen Mary*, which was permanently moored there, dining on fish, and chips fried traditionally the English way, with a side order of mushy peas, of course.

Our time passed very quickly in California and before long it was time to sail back; but, bizarrely – and unfortunately for the casino business – Mormons had chartered the ship, and they do not gamble. We opened our doors, but nobody came in, and we all got pretty bored. After dinner, the passengers basically retired to bed. The ship boasted good quality entertainment but due to non-attendance most of the shows were cancelled. The casino table's manager was a grumpy old man from Columbia. He had a very bad temper, and bad attitude generally, and things grew from bad to worse due to this total lack of business. By the time we arrived back at Miami things were so bad that many of the casino members, including me, could not handle him. Several of us decided to resign. I thought at the time I was making a bad mistake but – in solidarity and to make a point – we all stuck together in the forlorn belief that it would be the manager, not us, who would have to leave. But, as you can probably guess, this was not to be the case. We were out, and soon I found myself back on a flight to London. I arrived home a wiser man, perhaps, but certainly a very suntanned one, and excited to see my family and friends.

Europe

Once again here I was facing the big question – what was I to do now? I turned back to the entertainment business and fortunately a good friend, Greg Wilson, was organising a line up of DJs to go out to Europe to work in nightclubs. It was arranged for me to travel to Villers-Bocage in northern France to work in a brand new nightclub. I bought myself a beautiful white Jaguar and stacked high all my belongings and boxes of vinyl records roof high then said once again to my family and friends, "Au revoir." I purchased my one-way ticket for the Dover to Calais ferry and arrived in France rather tired but decided to drive straight on to my new nightclub.

I was very poorly prepared for this trip. For a start, I had brought no map, and little money either, as I was relying upon my negotiated weekly salary from the club. After several hours driving, and getting myself thoroughly lost on the pretty little French roads, I eventually found the town and then the nightclub. This, however, was only to find that they were even more unprepared for me.

I parked up and went inside and to my utter shock and dismay the club was only half built! Carpenters, electricians and bricklayers were all applying their respective trades and when I asked them the whereabouts of the club manager, they didn't have a clue. Apart from one stony face middle-aged Frenchman, nobody spoke a word of English. We muddled through with this guy's bit of English and me speaking "Desperanto", and the upshot was that, "Le club would not be ready for one month and 'le directeur' would not be around for a week or so." I was doubly scuppered – here I was, in France, on the understanding my food and lodgings were all included, plus weekly pay. I was running short on money, the daylight was fading. I know I should have not relied so much on the promises made, but it is only such experiences which teach us caution, or at least it was only such events that taught me not to be too trusting next time.

Do I stay or do I go? I was in a strange country with no accommodation and completely unfamiliar with the French people and the French language. It all looked as if it would be a great place but I had only the petrol in my Jag's two tanks and no money for the ferry ticket home. So, sadly, I made the decision to head back home. I arrived at the harbour and after explaining my situation to a pleasant English bloke who was an employee of the ferry company, they allowed me to use the company phone to ring home and get my parents to wire the money to purchase the ferry ticket. It would be two days before the ticket money would reach me and then there was the problem of getting from southern England to home.

Then the whole experience got really educational with two very uncomfortable nights sleeping rough, upright in my car. It's amazing how quickly a car gets cold once you switch the engine off. Then I learnt about the basic necessities of life as the small change I had left in my pocket bought me a packet of biscuits, a bottle of water and a bottle of Pernod. Maybe not everyone's choices but they worked for me that night.

Trying to pass the time as best I could, I went walking around the town and heard music emanating from a nightclub. This club was flakier than the one I came for, but at least it had a roof and walls and things. On the off chance, I went in and asked to speak to "Le directeur". So, I had learned some things already. This French guy spoke good English and when I explained my situation, he said, "If you DJ here tonight I will supply all your drinks on the house." I had nothing to lose and spent two nights working this rather horrible seedy venue. I was offered the DJ residency but I declined his offer as all I wanted was to get back to England. I arrived home at 8.30 in the morning, just in time for one of my mum's tasty bacon sandwiches and a hot mug of sweet tea. I was so exhausted I just wolfed breakfast and went straight to bed, sleeping the whole day and night.

I needed a job and, it has to be said, I was also missing the cruise ship lifestyle, so I decided to explore my options. I was given the phone number of a company named Southern Club Games, based in Southampton. After a lengthy conversation with the managing director, David Smith, it transpired they were in desperate need of a technician in Greece and a hurried interview for the following day was arranged for me. I made my way to Southampton by train. This time I took more money! I had learned that lesson, and this trip was much more comfortable and more relaxed. After an hour's interview, I was offered the job, on condition I would fly out in two days time. I agreed, and with a handshake and a signed contract, I travelled home with a big smile on my face, ready to explore Greece.

I arrived in Athens at two o'clock in the morning. No one was there to meet me, so of course, once again, I thought, is this going to turn out to be another nightmare, like in France? I had an address and showed it to a cab driver who spoke no English and with gestures, and more Desperanto – the Greek version that I invented on the spot – I asked him to deliver me there. After fifteen minutes driving, I arrived at the address and knocked on the door. A few minutes later, the door opened and the office secretary appeared in a very loose fitting dressing gown. She had fallen asleep and it was her job to pick me up. She beckoned me in and gave me her sincere apologies for her non-attendance at the airport. She introduced herself as Christine, from Australia, and, after a couple of glasses of wine and the company profile chat, she showed me to a bedroom and the nicely made up bed beckoned me to take some sleep.

Christine woke me around eight o'clock with tea and toast and said, "Everybody at the office is looking forward to meeting you," which was encouraging after France, so after a brisk shower and shave I was off to meet my new colleagues at Southern Club Games, Greek Division. Alekos Mavricos was the area director and I found him to be a complete gentleman. He told me of my position and duties and that I was to move in two weeks to Patras, on the Greek mainland, and I was to live in the Patras Palace, a five star hotel. My duty was to board the ferry and cruise ships in which my company operated the on board casino concessions in order to count the floats and repair any machines that had broken down on the previous sailing. It was also my duty to bank the money on the mainland. I then realised why the company required me to start at such short notice. It transpired that the previous company representative had absconded with the entire takings!

I made good use of my time before I transferred to Patras. During the office hours, I was escorted by a Greek engineer around the main port of Piraeus. I was amazed at the sheer size of the port and the amount of ships it contained. Outside office hours, Christine very kindly showed me the sites of old and new Athens, and I was a perfect tourist. One night, she took me to the famous Acropolis sight and sound show. We were driven out into the night and told to sit on certain benches in what seemed to be the middle of nowhere, no lights for miles, and the guide walked off. I said to Christine, "I think we have been literally taken for a ride here." She just laughed and said, "Alan wait and see." After what seemed like ages, the countryside suddenly lit up and I witnessed the fantastic history of ancient Greece in a sound and light presentation – it was wonderful.

Two weeks passed pretty fast. I was then driven to Patras and introduced to my contacts. I settled in very quickly in this small sleepy town and I realised I had a lot of free time to myself. But free time is a double-edged sword and after the first month I became very bored. I used to buy the English newspapers to catch up with events back home. One day, whilst reading the Daily Express, I read the headline, "Fashion Show at Olympia". I must have been in a trance – I knew there was a bus service which left for Olympia every hour, so I decided to go to Olympia and see this English show. I boarded the bus and before long I arrived at this beautiful archaeological site. I was still in a trance state when I entered a small tourist shop and asked the assistant where the fashion show was being hosted. In clear English, he informed me that he had traded in Olympia for many years and could tell me that no fashion show was being held in Olympia or ever would be.

It's embarrassing to describe now but even then it took a moment for the penny to drop and I froze to the spot – the show was being held in Olympia, but Olympia in London. And if it took the Daily Express and a boredom induced daydream to get me out of Patras and bumble into this magical spot, I was eternally grateful, for I was to have one of the most wonderful days discovering the birthplace of the Olympic Games.

Some months had passed and I grew more and more bored of Patras. Beautiful as it was, by then I knew the town inside and out, and I felt trapped and lonely in its routine. A routine can soon become a rut and there was not enough here for this

The Amerikanis, viewed from Bluebeard's Castle, St. Thomas, V.I.

healthy if hyperactive young bloke. I called Alekos and gave him my notice to leave. I still wanted the same work but on the cruise ships again, and, to my surprise, he was expecting my call as, over the years, this position had seen many company representatives come and go. I was in for a great surprise when Alekos called me later that day and told me a vacancy had turned up working for another company in the Caribbean called Atlantic Associates. I was to fly immediately back to England for a week and then fly to Genoa in Italy to join my party ship,

Britannis, which was to sail to the Caribbean and start weekly cruises!

Caribbean Cruising

After a whirlwind trip home, I was travelling once again. I arrived in Genoa and had a few hours to spare, so I decided to do some sightseeing. It was my first time in Italy and I found it really interesting. I had lunch at a café that was occupied by a Nazi SS unit during the Second World War. Bullet holes were still in the wall where poor innocent people had lost their lives at the hands of those evil barbarians. The *Britannis* was a real party cruise ship, very similar in size and scope to the *Carnival* and *Mardi Gras,* but operated with a Greek captain and officers. The rest of the crew were multinational. The casino staff were again mainly British and American and I settled in pretty quickly with them.

Before long, I was working hard during the long days and enjoying great parties every single night of the week. The ship's weekly itinerary included Miami, Barbados, St Lucia, St Thomas and Puerto Rico. Near to the port in Puerto Rico was a flying school and I used to sunbathe by the pool and watch students learning to fly. I seemed to know quite confidently in myself that I was going to learn to fly one day. I just knew I would do it but I didn't know where or when. I am not suggesting that this was a direct premonition but there was a strange certainty about it, and no hint of a doubt. I did, indeed, eventually learn to fly, and even qualified as a captain, but it was a good few years later.

My two favourite restaurants at the time were Bluebeard's Castle in St. Thomas and the Scotch 'n' Sirloin in the La Rada hotel in Condado, Puerto Rico. Every week I would dine at these fabulous restaurants, and often while sipping my gin and tonic in the healthy warm Caribbean evenings, my mind would drift to imagine what my friends were doing back home in England. I often wished I could bring all my friends and family out to share these experiences but it was not possible at that time or destined to be. My Spanish had come on really well and I used to enjoy my Saturday night out in Puerto Rico, speaking with the locals after dinner, on to a casino to see how others operated, then on to a nightclub and return to the ship for an early morning sail. It was a great life, and I did appreciate it.

The *Britannis* had a sister ship called the *Amerikanis* and Atlantic Associates operated the casino concession on board. The operational set up on our ship was running very smoothly but it was a different story on board the *Amerikanis,* so I was transferred over to help sort out their problems. Their itinerary was similar to ours but it included Antigua. It wasn't long before we had sorted all the issues and my boss, John Klemmer, contacted me and asked me to call in to Castle Harbour casino in Antigua and help them to install several new Bally slot machines which they had purchased. I agreed and duly arrived and was greeted by the owner. I worked very hard the whole day setting up the machines and putting them on line and when it was time to leave to sail with my ship an associate of the casino held my arm firmly and said menacingly, "You will come here each week and sort out any problems that may arise." I stared at him speechless and left for my ship.

I thought long and hard about what was said to me and I made my decision not to go back again. I was helping them free of charge, and they expected me do it on a weekly basis – crazy! The following week, on arrival at Antigua, I decided to sunbathe on deck for the whole day, and an hour after arriving in port, the ship's public address system paged me – "Would the casino manager please report to the purser's office immediately." I ignored the request and the announcement went out every half hour for the rest of the day. Just as the ship was about to depart, I went to my office to prepare for work and, lo-and-behold, who was standing outside but my *amigo,* the "henchman". He grabbed me and pushed me against the wall, at the same time verbally abusing me, saying how much I do not want to get on the wrong side of "the company", which, of course, I immediately translated as the Mafia. I was shocked and, I must admit, slightly scared, but when I reported the incident to John Klemmer he was most reassuring. John told me to take a hundred dollars out of the casino float for my inconvenience and promised me I would not be troubled again. And, thank goodness, I wasn't.

Morocco

Another very serious life threatening incident happened while on a one-off cruise to Tangiers. We were informed by the captain to be very careful onshore, to stay in a group and not to travel alone. The casino staff grouped together and we decided to explore the city. As we disembarked there was a lot of touting going on with the locals but one native stood out and offered to give us all a guided tour for just one U.S. dollar each! We all agreed and said, "Okay, let's go. Where is your bus parked?" "Bus? Oh, no. No bus. This is walking tour," he replied. We all thought it was too suspicious to be true so we decided to find our own way around. Another lesson was learned that day, if something sounds too good to be true, then it probably is!

The further we walked into town, the more our captain's warning became forefront in our minds. This was a very unsafe and unsavoury place for tourists. The streets were very dirty and smelly with beggars everywhere. It was impossible to walk five yards without being hassled. Undernourished children, with their limbs twisted around at birth – and some with amputated arms and legs - lay on the ground begging. These children were apparently considered "lucky" as they were at an advantage over the regular beggars. They, or their guardians, usually received more money from the pity factor induced in the tourists. It was a very depressing and, at the same time, intimidating and scary place. From this moment in time I became very proud of my country, thankful and extremely grateful for its protection. I was holding slightly to the back of our group as we meandered through the smell of the unkempt streets when I noticed a young boy, aged about eight years old. He reminded me of my young brother, John, at home in England, except this poor little boy had rags for clothes, soiled and dirty, and he had been following us for some time. He was trying to beg money from the group, but we had been warned by an old American tourist on the boat not to give, the children did not benefit whatsoever from the money received, it all went to their keepers.

I was stunned to see that because the young child was being ignored by us, the man, who was obviously associated with the young child, walked in front of us and, like a play act, blatantly put a coin in the child's hand, strongly implying we should emulate his action and do likewise.

But by now our group was tiring with the afternoon heat and to get respite we entered a leather goods shop and stayed in there to lose the interest we had attracted. After several minutes, we left the store and were greeted by a large commotion filling the street. I enquired as to what was happening and was told by a group of tourists that a young boy had been picked up for no apparent reason and was kicked so hard he somersaulted and landed on his head in the gutter while the crowd just stood around watching. I had to pick up the young child. He was bleeding a heck of a lot from wounds on his head and the poor mite was terrified and crying heartfelt tears. I was able to nurse him for a couple of minutes and realised it was the same boy that had followed our group earlier. I could feel myself losing my temper, and when I asked who did this to the boy, a tourist pointed out a man standing not too far away. I recognised him instantly. It was, of course, the same guy that had been following our group earlier – and then I lost it completely. I put the boy down and went to pick a fight with this man – and by now an even larger crowd had gathered around – but I was so angry, I rushed at him and pushed him hard against the wall, put up my fists and shouted as loudly as I could. Using all the strongest words I knew, I invited him to "try me for size". Within a second, I was pinned up against the wall by several scruffy heavies and a cutthroat razor was held up hard against my throat. I was told in broken English to, "Go quietly away now, or you will die today!"

I knew one wrong move and I would have had my throat cut and very probably bled to death in that very street. I have thought this through so many times, trying to resolve the despair I felt at that moment, but there was really only one thing that I could do. Separated from my group, I would have been dead or damaged very quickly, and the boy would gain nothing. There is very, very little that any one person alone can do. And what I did then was all I could do. I said as calmly as I could, "Okay." I was quickly released and the press of bodies around me melted away into the crowd of grinning locals. I was left in a state of shock, icy cold in the heat of the afternoon. I was shaken and dejected. How I made my way back to the ship, I don't know, but I vowed never to return to that part of the world again. And I haven't.

It was time to move on. I had been "head hunted" and a new job offer was presented to work on a ferry cruise from Portland, Maine, to Yarmouth, Nova Scotia. I was to fly to Boston, Massachusetts, to meet the ship *MS Caribe*. She was having a major engine refurbishment and was due to set sail in two weeks. This time delay gave me the opportunity to get to know the crew on board, including the casino staff, and to give each Bally slot machine a thorough check through. The day arrived for us to sail, but when the ship's engines started for the first time, there was a large muffled bang, followed by a sickening shudder that shook the whole ship. The engine's crankshaft had snapped. This damage to a major component of the ship's transmission had serious implications for the company. To fix this, the engine had to be stripped out completely again; so, consequently, we spent a total of three months aboard the ship in East Boston on full pay!

I found Boston to be a fantastic place. The people are very friendly, and the restaurants and clubs are superb. I used to visit Quincy Market and Faneuil Hall, regularly including an English Pub, called Lord Bunbury's, where we used to overindulge in Watneys Red Barrel ale. I started this drinking fad probably out of a certain homesickness for the British pub, but before long several of the casino staff would become regulars at this watering hole and blame me for their hangovers the following day. I had made friends with another guy from Jamaica, named Raymond. Raymond often came out to party with us and on one particular night, after a good drinking session at our "pub", he decided to retire early. Normally, I would have returned with him. On his way home, he took a short-cut through a dangerous area in East Boston and was attacked by four guys, two white and two black. The muggers held him at gunpoint and relieved him of his watch, rings and all his money. Ray used to carry all his savings with him as he believed this was the safest option. It probably was for him. But I didn't carry much cash or valuables at all, and I wonder – with the benefit of hindsight, of course – if I hadn't had a narrow escape that night. For, if I had left with him and also been mugged at gunpoint, not having much cash on me, the consequences may have been very, very different.

I had a colleague that worked shifts with me in the casino. His name was Cliff Millinoski. Cliff was older than I and a native – from Milwaukee – and we became good friends. We would often sit for hours talking about one of our favourite topics – U.F.Os and alien abduction. These things had always fascinated me. Now, Cliff was an official American government officer and was trained to interview witnesses who had experienced sightings and close encounters. He had to inform his superiors of his location at all times, and if a problem occurred within his region, he was instructed by a certain government agency to "handle" the situation. He carried security clearance, and the official documentation that I saw gave him access and powers over the police in these special circumstances. I continually probed him for information but, as he was sworn to secrecy for American national security purposes, I managed only to get snippets of information out of him. Cliff informed me that the existence of alien beings on Earth was true beyond any reasonable doubt! It was the first time anyone had talked as directly as this to me, and I listened as much as I could. I took his ideas in but held them close to my chest. Unknown to me at the time, I was going to experience several strange incidents in the future, which we will get to later in this book.

I spent three great months in and around Boston. Eventually the ship was fit for purpose and it was time to go to work. The daily crossing took ten hours and once again we only operated when the ship was at sea. I had one day and night per week off and I could spend it either in Canada or the United States. I chose Portland, in Maine, as within an hour's driving distance was a holiday town called Old Orchard Beach. In the holiday season it is very popular with the French Canadian tourists. The resort is very similar to Blackpool, in Lancashire, and I made many friends and frequented many parties there.

After several months on the *Caribe,* on one particular day, the German captain came into the casino and told me to clean various parts of it. I informed him that I was not a cleaner but I would instruct the duty cleaner to do the job immediately. He did not want to accept this and repeated that he wanted *me* to do the cleaning. I could see this was a major "situation" arising and once again I informed him of my status as casino manager and not a cleaner. After several more requests from him, I could see this confrontation was going nowhere, and I was certainly not going to bend to this dramatic alteration to my job description. So I said to him, in certain unpleasant words, that if he want the casino cleaning he should do it his "bloody self", and then walked away as grandly as I could. I retired to my cabin but within the hour I was informed that I was fired. I departed the *Caribe* with many fond memories; I had made some good friends and had some very interesting experiences, but I did what I felt I should and maybe it was time to move to pastures new. A flight was arranged for me to fly from a local airfield in Maine, on to Boston, and then on again to London, but I decided I had a different agenda.

I landed at Boston and cancelled my flight to London, booking instead a flight to Miami – I decided I was going to have a vacation. I boarded the aircraft, and sitting in the aisle opposite to me was an extremely attractive American girl of a similar age to me. I noticed – as you do – that each time I looked in her direction, it seemed she was looking at me. After take-off, I caught her looking again, so I beckoned her to come and join me. Before I got the chance to speak, she apologised for staring at me and said, "I know you." I replied, "I really don't think so.

I am from England." She said, "Yes, I know. Your name is Alan, and you are from Liverpool!" I was taken off-guard. How could this girl know me? She introduced herself as Susan and she lived on Collins Avenue, Miami, with her sister. Susan then explained that she worked part-time in a restaurant that I used to frequent. She also told me I used to visit her restaurant with another guy from England, also named Alan – this being Alan Williams from Carnival Cruise Lines. This proves once again that it is a very small world in which we live. I had a very pleasant vacation with Susan and went back to England feeling fully refreshed, and, again, very suntanned.

As always, returning to England, it was lovely to see my family and friends again; but I was also noticing, and finding myself rather surprised to see, that not many things had changed at home. To me, people at home were still doing the same things and in the same way. In the time I had been travelling, I felt I had lived a lifetime of experiences, seen so many things, visited so many places and met lots of very interesting people. Most importantly, these experiences had changed me in the way I felt and the way I looked at things. I felt I had probably done more things in this short time than most people do in a lifetime. I truly believe the pathway I took changed my life. It had taught me respect and made me view the world in a very different way. I was so grateful and I was still only in my early twenties!

So, I made a phone call to Jeanette Stevens at Atlantic Associates and explained my situation aboard the *MS Caribe*. Shortly after which she got back to me and I was offered a position on board the Italian cruise ship *Oceanic*. Flights were sorted out and once again I was jetting off across the Atlantic to join the ship in New York. The itinerary included the Bermuda Triangle. We were to cruise weekly from New York to the Virgin Islands, to Bermuda, then back to *the Big Apple*. We spent much more time at sea, which meant more working hours, but, as ever, with cruising there was always time to party!

The *Oceanic* was a really friendly ship and I had many good times on board. I made friends with the ship's American doctor, David James. Dave and I had many things in common but, most of all – and best of all – we both enjoyed chasing girls and drinking beer, strangely enough. On one particular cruise, I received a telephone call from Dave. "Alan, get down to the hospital, I have a crazy story to tell you." Well, I love "crazy", so I hurriedly made my way to the hospital. "What's the story, Dave?" I enquired.

The ship had several swimming pools and one of the pools was for children only, usually accompanied by their mothers while their fathers were off somewhere. One guy had been hanging around the pool, showing off his muscles by exercising around the place. The swimming pool was, in its deepest part, two feet. So he thought he was very clever by diving in and aquaplaning the top of the water. Which, I suppose, is okay to do if your pool is land based. But, after several successful dives, he became a tiny bit complacent, and just as he dived without paying the proper attention, the ship rolled ever so slightly to starboard, causing the water to move over with the ship. The guy dived straight along the bottom of the empty pool, and as well as bumps, bruises and a much dented ego, he ripped open another vital part of his anatomy. Then the very same ladies who he had tried so desperately hard to impress with his physique, escorted him bleeding profusely to the hospital, where Dave treated him and inserted over twenty stitches – ouch!

My new cruise itinerary proved very interesting; in particular, New York and Bermuda. I had one full day each week in *the Big Apple* and enjoyed dining at all of the best known restaurants, browsing the fantastic shops and visiting the famous landmarks: the Empire State Building, Wall Street, the Statue of Liberty, and, of course, the *World Trade Centre*.

Bermuda, a British Colony, however, was one of my favourite islands. It was really lovely to see some familiar British stuff. I warmed immediately to these comforts, planted down in this tropical paradise. Many of the friendly local residents were also proud to have a genuine allegiance to the Queen and the royals, and it was really funny to see the uniformed British "Bobbies" wearing short trousers. Pleasant times were had in Bermuda. I loved exploring, including several really interesting dives on shipwrecks, and a visit to a complete replica of the Royal Crown Jewels, on display in a museum. For me, this perfect cruise itinerary proved short lived as the company, all too soon, required my services elsewhere, and it was shortly to be the beginning of the end of my cruising life. I was transferred to the Costa Line shipping company and, in particular, the "party" ship, *Carla C*.

The *Carla C* was operated by an Italian crew and was classed as a "fun ship". By now, I knew a lot of people in the casino and cruise industry and it took me no time at all to settle in. Here also was John Grey, a Scottish magician, who presented a brilliant cabaret illusion show. Unknown to me at the time, he would be partly responsible for stimulating an interest that would ultimately lead to my future profession as a comedy stage hypnotist!

We were sailing into Amsterdam and were to join in the ceremony of the crowning of Queen Beatrix of Holland. Queen Beatrix and her entourage were due to have drinks with other dignitaries on board our ship, and the security was very intense. We had three days to play in Amsterdam and then we were to fly back to England. I decided to see what I could of the city's sights, but unfortunately the students in Holland took the opportunity to riot and protest march at the same time as the royal ceremony was taking place. I got stuck in the middle of hundreds of youths smashing windows and overturning cars. A police helicopter hovered very low and the power of the craft's downdraft, mixed with the riot police's armed charges with batons and teargas, was a truly terrifying experience. Lots of us took temporary cover in a shop doorway, which started the problem. First, I was crushed in tightly by groups of protesters until I found it very hard to breathe with the teargas. Then, I had to run to try and re-join the crowd and keep up the pace, or I would fall into the hands of the authorities. Even though I was totally innocent, and at the time didn't even have a clue what it was all about, I did not want to be arrested or innocently battered. Truncheons don't really worry about whose head they crack. Eventually, I managed to escape down a side street and kept running like Forrest Gump until I was clear of the riot.

My three days in Amsterdam passed very quickly, but although I was unaware of it at the time, I would return to Amsterdam many more times. Deeper down, I was saddened, as it was dawning on me that this was probably going to be my last ever cruise ship. Like most of us, I feel things long before I understand them clearly, and I had very confused emotions about leaving all this behind. This profession and this wonderfully adventurous lifestyle had a lot of appeal to me. But, at the same time, I could feel a real groundswell of excitement at the prospect of what the universe had in store for me next.

Back home in England, these feelings finally settled themselves in a long dark night of self-examination. All night long, I rocked back and forth as I watched the hours tick by on my little, luminous alarm clock. The thoughts all revolved around where I felt I was, and where I felt I really wanted to be. By the time dawn finally broke, I knew that a change had occurred in my life. Something was about to begin, and without knowing just what it would be, I knew, at least, that I was ready.

CHAPTER FOUR
WIDE AWAKE

Settling in back home and re-adjustment was not easy at first. I had taken many things in life for granted and yet, once again, I was in another quandary as to what to do with my life. Before I left England for the United States, my entertainment opportunities as a DJ looked very promising. So I exerted myself and focused on this line of employment. I had made a very good choice. I auditioned for a large brewery chain of bars and won the audition and landed a string of bars that were very trendy at the time. Thank goodness I had landed on my feet again.

It was not long before I became firmly established and my services were in big demand and I could choose when and where I wanted to perform. The format and my style of presentation went from playing music in bars and nightclubs to acting in shows, compering big named acts and cabaret. It was this background in general entertainment that gave me the experience to be able to captivate a large paying audience that was essential for my future profession as a stage hypnotist and for the forthcoming paranormal shows.

Several notable experiences that are worthy of a mention during this period include accidentally setting fire to myself with petrol, shooting myself with a 9mm Uzi machine gun, getting buried alive in a real coffin six feet deep for charity and being a test dummy for a knife throwing magician. All these crazy episodes will be explained as you read on.

They all stem from a new concept born in Liverpool – Bonkers Show Bars. Bonkers was a new style of entertainment, and all the staff were employed not for pouring pints but for their entertainment skills. Every ten minutes something completely outrageous would happen. And by "outrageous" I mean riotous, risky and often downright dangerous. For example, the bar staff riding unicycles around the venue, volunteers testing their pain threshold on a bed of nails, naughty customers being locked in "*Ye Olde* medieval stocks" and tormented (sometimes undressed), acting out comedy sketches on stage, "phantom flan flingers" dressed as the Grim Reaper giving the customers cream pies in the face, yard-of-ale drinking competitions, and an amazing fire eating display which I presented. Anything and everything happened on our stage. The staff would rehearse during each day and perform every night. Due to the commercial success of Bonkers, other operators in the UK tried to emulate the concept, including a Bonkers in Ayrshire, Scotland. I was invited north of the border to perform for three nights and the following incident has been "burnt" into my memory literally and will never be erased.

On the first night we had staged several shows and it was now time for me to perform my fire eating routine. I had arranged for the local resident DJ to play my introduction and show music at the specific cue, giving me enough time to dress and prepare my fire sticks. During that day I was forced to purchase a can of petrol lighter fuel, as I could not source my usual slow burning white spirit. I had used petrol before and I knew it was very dangerous and extreme caution was needed when handling

Eating fire at a Masonic fund raising party

67

it. But just as I was finishing my preparation – and before the pre-arranged stage time – the DJ started my show introduction, taking me completely by surprise. I quickly soaked my fire sticks and took a mouthful of petrol straight out of the can. I had to drink the fuel out of the centre of the can and in doing so spilt the petrol down my face and neck. Without thinking this through properly and getting this stuff wiped off completely, I rushed to the stage, quickly placed on my mask and cape and walked out onto the stage with all tapers lit.

The house lights were down, the audience were all shouting and enthralled as I made my entrance. My fire sticks were glowing like a beacon on the dark stage as I blew out the petrol from my mouth to create the fire train. All too great effect but the residue petrol on my face caught fire and I went up in flames. Rupert, my colleague, who was dancing alongside, thankfully took control of the situation and pulled my black gothic cloak up and over my face to extinguish the flames. I was now really in a complete state of shock but the golden rule in show business is, "The show must go on!" So I continued the routine in this sort of subconscious auto pilot mode but as I drew the fire tapers near to my mouth, my face re-ignited once more. Thanks again to Rupert who by now was sticking close to me, monitoring my every move. He quickly extinguished my flaming face, but this time he carried me off stage into the dressing room. All the skin on the left hand side of my face, neck and ear had burnt off and I looked like the Phantom of the Opera when he takes his mask off. Fortunately, an off duty nurse was in the audience followed us into the dressing room and she took one look at me and said, "We need to get you to hospital." I was in a complete state of shock and still more concerned about the show than I was with my own health. But they insisted and I was taken to hospital. I was very fortunate that my burns were only superficial and within five weeks I was back to normal, fully recovered, with no scaring and still retaining my cheeky good looks! I just don't fire eat any more, I've lost my appetite for it.

One of my regular weekly residencies was at a cabaret nightclub in North Wales named Bentleys. One particular

Wednesday night I was on stage compering a stage hypnotist show when memories of the cruise ship days came flooding back to me. I was captivated by the entertainer's skills and I thought, "I could do this," and, please, without wanting to sound arrogant, I felt much, much better.

The die was now cast, knowing at this point in my life that my true vocation was opening up to me. I just knew it. I had such a strong feeling that something so big, so important and powerful was waiting just for me. The very next day I started my research; there was so, so much to do. I started studying long before the convenient tools of the internet were available, reading many books and researching anything and everything on hypnosis. I went to see one of the top performers of the day at the Empire Theatre in Liverpool, but even at this very early stage in my career, I knew that plagiarising other artists' work was totally taboo and unacceptable. I had to work hard and produce my own material and presentation.

Soon the time was right. I was confident with what I had learned. I was ready to cross the threshold, and all the hard work was ready to be put into practise on the stage. But where could I perform such a show?

One of my regular resident DJ nights was at a popular venue in the pleasant town of Hoylake, Wirral, named Flat Foot Sams, and it was here that I performed my first ever hypnotic induction and show. I kept calm, having already learned the craft to master a large crowd, I used my skills confidently and invited five willing volunteers on to the stage. Within minutes I had every one of them in a deep hypnotic trance. It was a tremendous feeling knowing that I could do it. I was so mentally engrossed with the induction that I almost forgot what I was going to do with them in the show. I demonstrated with a few simple comedy routines and then removed the trance state on the emphasised command of, **"WIDE AWAKE"**. The audience gave me a lovely round of applause and my night ended with me in a state of euphoria! I now knew where my future lay but how was I to get established and at the same time maintain some sort of a regular income?

It worked out that remaining in the clubs and running both professions in parallel – though keeping the work separate and distinct – was the only balanced way forward.

It was around this time that I lost another one of my nine

Captain Bates with Cessna G-BEWR, Liverpool

lives and now, looking back, I can see how foolish and stupid I was. A friend of mine, Steve, had a hobby – firearms – and he was a member of a local gun club. Before the tragedy of the Scottish Dunblane school massacre, he legally owned an Uzi nine millimetre machine gun, just like Arnold Schwarzenegger used in his Hollywood films. I was really keen to see it and to fire off a few rounds, just to say that I had fired an Uzi machine gun. So he brought it to my home, the Old School House. For safety reasons, he emptied the magazine with the exception of one round and allowed me to fire it off into my courtyard wall at point blank range. We thought it was safe to do so as it was not in a public place and was totally sheltered – nobody could be harmed. Or so we thought. The Great Architect of the Universe must have been taking care of me again that day because, as I pulled the trigger, the nine millimetre bullet ricocheted off the facing wall, its trajectory pointing at me, and it shot past my arm, burning it as it touched the skin before embedding into the wall behind me. It was a very, very close call. Those big bullets don't take prisoners. It has left a small scar on my left forearm but once again I had dodged the "Grim Reaper". I kept the spent brass cartridge on my key ring as a souvenir for a long time, and would still have it now but I had to surrender it to security one day at an airport as I boarded a flight.

Author as Margaret Thatcher, John Cecchini as Ronald Reagan, waterskiing at Hoylake

It was about this time that I fulfilled a dream I had had since I was a boy. On 19th July, 1983, I made a decision to learn to fly. My memories of sunbathing on board the cruise ship watching trainee pilots taking off and landing circuits in Puerto Rico flooded my head so I had my first introductory flight in a Cessna fixed wing aircraft, registration G-FAYE. The flying club was based at Liverpool's John Lennon Airport, formally Speke Airport. And after just one lesson I was completely hooked.

My flying instructor was Paul Dickinson and his father Dennis was the owner of the flying club, CATS (Cheshire Air Training School). He was also the Chief Flying Instructor (CFI). I received immense pleasure from learning to fly. There was so much to learn, and over a period of time I managed to pass all my exams including, radio telephony (RT), air frames and aero engines, air law, air navigation and a general flying test. My first solo flight took place on 16th September, 1983. The CFI flew with me prior to the solo and we practised several circuits, or "touch and go" as we then called them. And then, totally unexpectedly to me, he received air traffic control clearance to stop on runway 27's fast

71

turn off, this is a short cut on the runway back to the apron. He opened the aircraft door, jumped out and said, "You're on your own son. Good luck." I was shocked. I knew I was ready for a solo flight but I didn't know when it would happen. It was just like a game of Russian roulette. After a successful circuit, a smooth landing and a debrief back at the hangar, I received the following certificate:

Hear ye, Hear ye, and take heed that on this most memorable 16th day of September in the year 1983 Alan Bates was duly released from the verbal bonds of his instructor and authorised to take off on a first solo flight in a Cessna flying machine, registration G-FAYE and indeed after circumnavigating the airfield at Liverpool did land again proving once more the third law of Sir Isaac Newton. To any disbeliever, this scroll shall bear witness to the courage, skill and good fortune of the holder, in his moment of glory signed with shaking pen, Alan Bates and the CFI.

The 19th October, 1984, was a very proud day for me and my family. I received my pilots licence – Captain Bates, licence number PP36394A, and my treasured "wings".

Apart from the thrill of my flight training, and flying in general, one of my memorable experiences was while piloting an aeroplane from an ex-RAF World War Two base, Swanton-Morley, near Norwich, into RAF Duxford. As I joined the circuit for landing, the air traffic controller advised me that I was number three in traffic to land and, for my visual VFR information, the aircraft at number two was a Spitfire, lining up for final approach! It was an honour just to share some of that legendary aircraft's airspace and, particularly, to land with it at Duxford, where the valiant units of Hurricanes and Spitfires of the "Big Wing", as they called it, flew from during the Battle of Britain.

By now I was on the books of several entertainment agencies and was starting to get a lot more work. Both of my professions were in steady demand, which kept me very busy travelling the length and breadth of the United Kingdom. I was also broadcasting a weekly radio show on Radio Mersey Waves, which I enjoyed immensely but I knew that the only way of really progressing was to present a regular successful show on national television.

My first TV appearance was on *Up Front*, with regional Granada Television, broadcast live from Manchester. The show was presented by the talented Lucy Meacock and the colourful character Tony Wilson (now sadly missed). Tony was a Northern music mogul and the founder and owner of the world famous Manchester nightclub, The Hacienda. I enjoyed my first taste of television in that illustrious company, and it wasn't long before lots more was to come my way, including one of my favourites, *Xarabank*, in Malta, to which I have dedicated a separate chapter. My reputation and experience was now growing and the next stage forward was the theatre. I embarked on a theatre tour initially around the North West of England and, shortly after, nationally. The big difference between working on television and performing to a live theatre audience is the atmosphere. The pure adrenaline rush that one gets treading the boards backstage, or in the wings waiting to go on, I compare to Roman times, when gladiators were to face combat in the arena. If this feeling could be bottled and sold it would be the bestselling "high" on the market.

My first primetime TV slot was on "That's Life", presented by Esther Rantzen, Gavin Campbell, Doc Cox and Adrian Mills. The show was broadcast live nationally every Saturday evening and the ratings were phenomenal, in many, many millions. The reason for my invitation onto this show was quite a tale, the result of a radio interview I gave on my local radio station in Liverpool, Radio City.

I was giving a late-night interview to help promote ticket sales for my live show at the Neptune theatre in Liverpool (now re-named the Brian Epstein theatre, after the famous Beatles manager) when a lady named Clare rang the studio and asked if it was possible to hypnotise dogs, as her pet Doberman,

"Sabre", was barking so much during the night and disturbing the neighbours that she was considering having him put to sleep.

I knew that during the 1960s, animal psychologists had obtained good results in cognitive behavioural training similar to Ivan Pavlov, the famous Russian physiologist, while studying digestion in dogs. As a big animal lover, and under those circumstances, I had to offer to help, and arrangements were made off-air to visit and see what I could do. I met with the family, and of course Sabre, a lively but lovely animal who took an instant liking to me. I was left with him for thirty minutes and I managed to calm him down and, I believe, communicate with him. As daft as it sounds, it seemed to work as, the following week, Clare returned back on the radio and sincerely thanked me.

I thought this would be the end of the matter but not so; the UK press got hold of the story and it went international. Every newspaper, radio station, local, national and international wanted the story, and this was the reason I was invited onto the TV show, *That's Life*. The story got even better when I arrived as the reason why they wanted me live on the show was because the week before my Sabre story broke they had a gentleman on the show from Southern England who lived with fourteen dogs in a small semi-detached house; and, likewise with Sabre, the neighbours were going crazy with the noise. There was one particular dog named Squibb that would not stop barking, and so, of course, they wanted me to hypnotise her live on national TV! They brought Squibb on to the set and she lived up to her reputation of aggression and loud barking. Luck was certainly with me that evening as given ten minutes with Squibb, I had managed to calm her down to such an extent that she fell asleep. If the truth be known, I was terrified on set because at one point I was convinced that I was going to be really badly bitten.

The one and only dog I ever had was Trixie. Trixie was a cross between an Alsatian and a Labrador, and without doubt was a true and faithful companion that accompanied me everywhere I went. I found her in a rescue home. I just knew she had a beautiful nature and during our time together she never required a name collar. She did not need one as she never ever left my side. It is a different kind of love that you have for your dog and Trixie gave me her all. She was totally, 100 percent, dedicated to me and imposed no restrictions on her love; and my feelings for her were mutual. Any dog owner reading this will understand the very special and unique bond that exists between a dog and a human.

When she was a young pup, I used to take her for exercise to my local beach. During my busy periods I would let her out of the car, and after half an hour of hectic fun and charging about, she had had her daily exercise. We jumped back in the car and off we went together on our busy schedule.

One day, I let Trixie out of the car at the beach and all went well until towards the end of her workout she inadvertently charged full tilt into the back of the car. Maybe she was overexcited and misjudged her distances, or I was preoccupied with work and wasn't watching, but there was a loud thump and everything went quiet. Walking around the car, I saw her lying still on the ground. I feared the absolute worst and ran over to her. It was my worst nightmare. She was my best and closest friend. But as I got to her, she began yelping, obviously in lots of pain, but at least she was alive. I picked her up and with tears in my eyes placed her on the front seat before driving like a maniac to the local vets surgery. She was immediately attended to and I was informed that the next twenty four hours would be crucial.

Luckily, after many stitches and a night stop over at the surgery, thankfully she survived. I picked her up the next day and brought her home, cuddling up to her all day and night in my bed. The next day, when I gave her a bowl of warm milk, she lifted her head off my pillow and out came the long tongue to drain the bowl dry. Within an hour, she was fit as a fiddle, but played on me for attention all day. That was the last time Trixie exercised in that manner. The saying, "a dog is a man's best friend", is very true. Sadly, many years later, on Saturday, 4th August, 2001, Trixie, my best friend and companion for thirteen years, had to be put to sleep. It was one of the worst days in my life. This was not the last time I would see Trixie – she came back to visit me as a ghost and I have fully covered the story in the chapter, "The Spirit World".

Over time I have given many interviews and guest appearances on lots of various TV shows, local, national and international, including another primetime UK show, Joan Bakewell's *Heart of the Matter*, on the BBC. Other shows have included *The Graham Norton Show*, Ireland's *The Saturday Night Show* on primetime RTE, presented by Brendan O'Connell, *The Friday Night Show* with James Whale, and many numerous other documentaries and chat shows.

During a theatre tour of Mumbai, India, in May 2011, my TV shows reached a record number of viewers, over one billion, while filming with UTV World Movies, achieving the status of the most broadcast hypnotist in TV history! Likewise, I was the first hypnotist to be broadcast on a live national TV show in Kuala Lumpur, Malaysia, in 2014.

I have also produced and pitched several pilots for TV shows and commercials, including one particular audition for a TV commercial advertising, of all things, butter. The producers wanted a natural "wow factor" expression on people's faces when they tasted the product, and to get this they chose David Blaine, the American magician, in New York, and myself, in London. Part of the filming was to go out on the streets of London, hypnotise people, then suggest to them that when I clicked my fingers on the command of **"WIDE AWAKE"**, my head would come off my shoulders – they would then film the "wow factor" expression. It really did work and I was very, very pleased with my results. However, David "across the pond" in New York, received an even bigger "wow factor" when he performed his levitation illusion on the streets of "the Big Apple" and won the contract for the commercial. It was close and fairly balanced but I was happy to have had the experience and the audition.

My DJ, show acting and general entertaining were still important factors in my life. While performing weekly at a venue named Evergreens in Stoke on Trent, Staffordshire, I agreed to be buried in a coffin, six feet deep, for one day, to raise money for Barnardos, a children's charity. My brother John and I set in place plans that would ensure that I would survive the claustrophobic box that would be my resting place for the designated time underground. The burial would take place on Monday 28th August, 1989, at noon.

At exactly midday the lid was sealed on the coffin and I was lowered into the cold bosom of the earth, a eulogy was read out by my friend, DJ Jacko, dressed as a vicar. I started to panic but luckily I managed with self-control

Author & Graham Norton, "Green Room", 2007

to get the better of my feelings. The worst part of the whole experience was listening to the sound of the soil being shovelled onto the coffin lid by the grave diggers until the muffled sound disappeared; I was on my own, in pure serene silence. Once settled, I could control the compressed fresh clean air that was supplied to me by a compressor on the surface, diligently operated by my brother John. I had a headstone and flowers placed on my grave and by now the very large gathering of people there to witness my burial had now disappeared to the bar. I will give you one guess only to who was left mourning at my graveside. Throughout the ordeal, sitting and whimpering at the grave, was Trixie, my dog!

If you were to lock your wife and your dog in the boot of your car for one hour, when you opened the boot, who do you think would be really glad to see you? Such is the love of your dog.

I was successfully exhumed at six o'clock in the evening, as planned, and the large crowd had returned to witness my resurrection. During my restful time in the coffin, I had a telephone link to BBC Radio Staffordshire, and they were broadcasting live my progress on the hourly news, thus creating even more interest. But, more importantly, the voyeurs and curiosity seekers were donating more money to Barnardos charity! I managed to change clothes in the coffin before the resurrection, so when the coffin lid was removed, I was dressed with a skull and skeletal costume which gave the spectators quite a shock! I did not know at the time but I would repeat this daring stunt again for another charity in Malta in 2002, and it would be televised but on a much grander scale.

There was an extremely sad ending to working at this wonderful venue. The original management team, Liverpudlians Ronnie and Jacky James, left to return to work in a new venue in Paradise Street, Liverpool. After a short while at their new premises, an intruder stayed hidden in the bar after closing time, and Ronnie discovered him – his intentions were to steal the contents from the safe. Knowing Ronnie as I did, this would not have been acceptable, and Ronnie paid with his life, stabbed sixteen times. His blood-soaked body was discovered shortly afterwards by his wife Jackie. The murderer was eventually apprehended by the diligent work of Merseyside police, convicted, and is now justly serving life imprisonment.

Have you ever been on holiday and met likable holidaymakers whom you have struck up a rapport and made friends with? I am sure you have. Did you ever give them your business card, knowing that you will never see them again? I am sure you have. To celebrate my birthday, my girlfriend Alnifa and I went on a cruise on Egypt's River Nile. We visited the popular tourist sites, including the Cairo Museum, the pyramids, the Valley of the Kings and Queens, Aswan Dam and, the highlight, Abu Simbel. It was an amazing experience and whilst on board the cruise ship I met Argyle Miles from Sydney, Australia. Argyle was aged in his seventies and he proved to be one of the most memorable and inspirational characters I have ever met. When we disembarked the ship at the end of our holiday to return to England, I gave Argyle my telephone number, instructing him to call me if he ever visited the North West of England, deep down believing the chances were very remote. I was to be proved very wrong.

Several months later, Alnifa and I had sadly ended our relationship, and one day, out of the blue, I received a telephone call from a crazy sounding Australian. It was Argyle and he was visiting Liverpool, just for a few days only, on his "European tour" – very brave for a man in his mid-seventies, I must add. I invited him to dinner and suggested he stay for the evening as, after a good meal and several large Scotch whiskies, I thought it unfair for him to have to drive back to a strange city. Argyle assessed my personal situation and took it on his shoulders to be my personal butler, chef, dog walker, cleaner and, most importantly, a friend. He did not want payment and stayed at my home rent free for over five months! Argyle eventually completed his tour of Europe and called me several times while backpacking in the snowy Alps in wintertime. The last I heard from him, he was in great fitness and his new job was delivering meals on wheels to "the elderly" back in Australia (while in his late eighties!).

The common cliché "nothing lasts forever" is very true. All good things must come to an end and my DJ entertaining days were drawing to a close. I knew in my heart; it was just like the feelings I held in Amsterdam at the end of my cruising days. It had come full circle, coincidentally after a stint in Liverpool. I basically started my career in the holiday town of New Brighton, Wirral, at the Penny Farthing, and I completed my last ever gig next door in the Playas Lounge, New Brighton. The industry had been very kind to me and I am forever grateful for all the friends and lovers I made on the way, and for all the amazing experiences.

All my energies were now going into performing hypnotic stage shows and the demand for overseas touring was increasing. I was invited to travel and tour the Arabian Gulf states, including Dubai, Al Ain, Sharjah, Doha, Abu Dhabi and Bahrain, along with my dear friend from Liverpool, the comedian Gary Skyner. We sold out every venue and successfully helped launch the Dubai Company, Laughter Factory. I returned to tour Dubai every year for the following ten years. Gary was born disabled and has very

short arms and missing fingers due to the disastrous effect of the drug, Thalidomide, which was prescribed for expectant mothers with morning sickness. His opening line on stage at our very first show was, "Good evening, ladies and gentlemen, and welcome to the Hyatt Hotel.

Comedian Gary Skyner, minder Jimmy, and author, on tour in Dubai

It's nice to be here in Dubai, but it's the last time I go f*****g shoplifting!" (Insinuating the authorities had cut his arms off for stealing). Gary lifted the roof off the ballroom with the applause he received, he was such a joy to be around; he exuded happiness and laughter everywhere he went, on and off the stage.

While we were shopping at a mall, Gary directed my attention to a particular store, The Body Shop, looking through the window and beckoning me in. As soon as I entered, I instantly knew he was up to no good. There were two pretty young Asian girls serving behind the counter and when they saw Gary their jaws dropped. Thalidomide was covered up in the Middle East and it would have been their first experience seeing a victim. When Gary broke the silence and asked them for "two elbows and three fingers please," the poor girls were totally speechless. Gary said to them with a straight face, "What's wrong, ladies? This is the Body Shop, isn't it?" [1]

During my career, I have helped and assisted many, many charities in raising funds for all types of good causes. The story I now tell has rather an eerie ending.

Ricky Tomlinson, author, Pauline Daniels & Stan Boardman, charity fundraiser

In March 2012, I was asked by Gary to help raise funds for the James Bulger memorial fund in Liverpool. James was a two year old boy who was abducted and tragically murdered, his battered body left on a railway line in Bootle, Liverpool, in February 1993. Such was the gruesome nature of the murder, it drew world attention and will never ever be forgotten on Merseyside. In association with James's mother, Denise, Gary had put together a package of wonderful entertainment, and all the proceeds went to the memorial fund. Artists and guests included stars of UK stage and screen, such as Ricky Tomlinson, Pauline Daniels, Stan Boardman, Paul Boardman, Paul Debek, the famous opera singers from the TV show *The X Factor*, and, of course, myself.

As I write this chapter Gary is now on day 22 of a hunger strike in a protest against the German pharmaceutical company, Grunenthal. He is protesting in hopes of a financial settlement for all the victims of the thalidomide tragedy and he intends to go all the way. My sincere and heartfelt support goes out to him and to the thousands of sufferers worldwide.

On the way to the show, I passed through a part of Liverpool that I would not normally travel. As I had time on my hands, I detoured slightly and went to visit the grave of a friend's wife, Karen. Karen was an extremely beautiful young lady, both inside and out, but, due to troubles unknown, she had hung herself from a tree in Liverpool. I attended the grave, paying my silent respect before continuing on to the fundraiser.

The next evening, I was to perform at Derek Acorah's annual fan club dinner in Coventry and, after the performance, my attention was peculiarly drawn to an old lady sitting on her own. I decided to strike up a conversation with her and, after a few minutes, she told me that she was a witch and professed to have strong powers. She now had my full attention, especially when she asked if I had been to visit a young female's grave recently. I froze to the spot and when I regained my senses I told her I had. The witch proceeded to describe the manner of her death, leaving me with very disturbed emotions on my long drive home.

Overseas performances had now become a regular part of my business. During the next few years, I would travel and perform in Luxemburg, Germany, Spain, India, Uganda, Cairo, Bali, USA, Switzerland, Ireland, Singapore, Malaysia and Brunei. I have set aside a chapter, "By Royal Appointment", specifically to cover my visit to Brunei.

In 2012, I had the privilege to perform at the Jakarta, Indonesia, Fringe Comedy Festival which gave me the opportunity to work alongside some of the very best and most famous comedians in the world. The headline act was Bill Bailey. I also had the great pleasure to work with northern comedian Peter Kay from the popular TV sitcoms, Phoenix Nights and Car Share.

We performed together at the University Great Hall, Exeter in June 2001.

During our stage and sound check rehearsals I was sharing the stage with Indonesia's famous magician and crazy illusionist, Deddy Corbuzier. Deddy had set up a large backdrop and when I asked him what he was using it for he replied, "It's for my knife throwing routine." He then asked if he could practise on me. Perhaps he hypnotised me because I immediately replied, "Yes, sure." I stood against the board and in seconds – bang, bang, bang, bang

Knife throwing target on stage, Jakarta

– four very sharp knives were embedded, two a centimetre away from each of my temples and two equally as near to my "privates". I came out of my trance state very quickly thinking, "What on earth did I say 'yes' for!" If I had moved just a fraction, it would have been fatal. The knives in the picture were positioned later for the camera pose. I later sold the rights of my show to Indonesian television and consequently my show was edited, subtitled and broadcast nationally, I believe, throughout Indonesia.

During one performance at the popular Warbler club and hotel in Bahrain, I noticed an Arabic gentleman in traditional dress, sitting at a table on his own watching the show. I remember thinking, "I wonder who he is?" The Warbler was generally an exclusive member's club, attended by westerners, the United States Navy and the British Royal Air Force. I was so busy with my show that I never gave it a second thought. At the end of the show, Amitabh, the general manager, said, "The hotel owner wants to speak with you." I changed and went to his office. He said, "Good evening, Mr. Bates, the prince of the ruling Bahrain royal family was most impressed by your

Author & Bill Bailey, Jakarta Comedy Festival

presentation this evening and has invited you and your wife, Michelle, for lunch at the palace tomorrow, and hopes you will be able to accept his invitation." Michelle, who was standing just behind me at the time, nearly fell over with shock. Her first words were quite typical of most women. "Oh my Gosh, what will I wear?"

The next day, we met for lunch. We were joined by HRH the Prince and Princess of Bahrain, and the princess's father, who was the ex-ambassador to the United Kingdom and a personal friend of Her Majesty the Queen. Michelle and I were rather nervous and apprehensive at the beginning but, as lunch progressed, all our pre-lunch nerves had disappeared and we truly enjoyed their company. During our dessert course, our lunch hosts were laughing rather loudly as I was telling a story, and when I enquired what was wrong, they laughed even more. It turned out that while I was eating my cream meringue nest I had a really big blob of cream on my nose. Michelle and the royal party deliberately did not tell me and were giggling amongst themselves. We finished our lunch and thanked our hosts for their good company and fine hospitality and were driven back to our hotel.

In November 2001, I was delighted to be invited to perform

a show in Kampala, in the Republic of Uganda, East Africa, on the occasion of the celebration of the Royal Society of St George. Andrew, the organiser, greeted me at the airport and took me straight to the venue where I was to perform. The venue was an upmarket restaurant in Kampala, named Mateus. I was informed it would be fully attended, virtue of the fact that, as in Andrew's own words, "they were starved of entertainment". The majority of the audience was English; but, amongst the guests, nationalities also included Scottish, Irish, American and Australian. The guest of honour was the British High Commissioner, and I was to be seated next to him for dinner.

The next morning, I was to prepare for the show early. We went to the venue and completed the sound checks and, in general conversation on the subject of safety in the area, I was informed, "Don't worry, Alan, you will be safe." Ten minutes later, I overheard a conversation discussing just how many armed guards would be required and where they would be positioned. When Andrew had finished his conversation, I quizzed him again on security issues, and he said, "Due to the nature of our gathering, and the presence of the British High Commissioner, we require protection, and that was why the location had been kept a secret and the event was not printed on any advance invitations."

After sound checks were completed, I went back to my hotel to rest. In the early evening, I was picked up and chauffeured back to the venue, and I was very surprised to see the road blocked off with armed guards in uniform everywhere – the remaining parked cars in the area were being examined for bombs. I had to run the gauntlet to get inside; I was searched, my name confirmed on the guest list, and only then was I allowed to pass freely.

I was introduced to the British High Commissioner and took my seat at the table next to him, but due to my pre-show nerves, I had no appetite whatsoever. (With hindsight, I was glad I didn't have an appetite.) The evening menu sounded delicious, smoked fillets of Nile perch, served on a bed of lettuce with dill sauce, medallions of beef served with a Hollandaise sauce, and, for desert, brandy truffles served with sauce Anglaise. When the main course was served, the caterers had dropped a major clanger – the kitchen staff had served *all* the beef medallions with sweet custard instead of Hollandaise sauce! The look on the guests' faces as they took their first bite was very amusing. The show passed off without a hitch.

The 9th December, 2010, was a particularly interesting month with an event that I will always remember. I travelled to Germany and performed a pre-Christmas show for the British troops based at Falling Bostal, near Bremen. The show was for the 16 Tank Transporter Squadron RLC. I was met at the airport by British army soldiers in uniform and driven to the base. After strict admission security checks, I was taken to the barracks and to the room where I would be sleeping for the night. It felt surreal as the room I slept in would have been occupied by a German officer in 1944. The show was well received by over one hundred excited squaddies – who really knew how to enjoy themselves – and they were a delight to work with. My flight the following day was in the evening so I had the full day on my hands for exploring. I was asked if I would like a British army "special" tour around Bergen-Belsen concentration camp. I accepted, not knowing what to fully expect, but on our arrival it was snowing very heavily and we were greeted by a deathly silence – no birds singing in the woods. Nothing. There was a distinct sadness around the whole area, and during my visit I was left for a while to reflect on the poor souls that perished in this terrible place.

Belsen brought back memories of visiting Anne Frank's house in Amsterdam. I realised that she had died within the walls of this camp, in March, 1945, and within my sightline, though in an unmarked grave, along with fifty thousand innocents. I was also taken to the building and site where Schindler's List was filmed.

In November 2014, I was invited for the second time to perform in Kuala Lumpur, Malaysia.[2] Hypnosis and, indeed, comedy hypnosis, were virtually unknown throughout this Muslim country, so when I performed live, the locals were totally blown away. After my first stage show, I took a bow, followed by an encore – and just as I was leaving the stage, a man cornered me, took out his wallet, emptied it, and demanded that I take all his money. I replied that I could not possibly do such a thing, but my management, while escorting me off the stage, quietly whispered, "Take it, otherwise it would be considered an insult." (I did not hypnotise him – honestly.) Reluctantly, I took the money, (a considerably large amount) and the stranger complimented me by saying he had had the best night's entertainment in his life. I was told upon reaching the dressing room that the man was a very wealthy, and important person politically, and held the title "Datuk", which is an equivalent to a knighted "Sir" in the UK. I passed on the money to my Singapore management team and asked them to donate the money given to a Malaysian charity.

As a born entertainer, I just really love working the stage. I never tire of it. But for several years now, I have been drawn to helping people with their psychological problems. I suppose it started while I was filming a pilot TV show in October 2004 named *Be Careful What You Wish For*. One of the producers had a serious migraine and was finding it difficult to focus. As with all television work, there is a lot of waiting time, so I asked if I could help her. My offer was accepted and I managed to place the lady in a light state of hypnosis very quickly and then to successfully remove the migraine. I really enjoyed being able to give the lady relief and I felt a great deal of satisfaction afterwards.

Another die was now cast in my life – hypnotherapy – to which I have dedicated a chapter.

[1] *Gary Skyner's book, "Turned a Tear into Triumph", by Gary Skyner and Dave Sampson, is available in bookshops and online.*

[2] *My Malaysian manager and promoter Steven Joseph passed away with a heart attack several weeks after this tour, sadly missed.*

CHAPTER FIVE
BY ROYAL APPOINTMENT

Early hours on the 1st April, 1992, I was awakened with an overseas telephone call. The call felt particularly loud, and my head was still spinning and dizzy from a really good party that I had attended earlier. The line was rather poor and the voice on the other end said, "Alan, its Crystal. I am calling from Brunei and I have an important gig for you." My brain began then to engage as the excited voice continued. "Alan, listen to me. The American singer and showman, MC Hammer, has let Princess Hamidah down on her fifteenth birthday party and they need a replacement act pretty quick. I put your name forward and they have accepted." I was totally confused and Crystal needed answers right away. Luckily, my immediate answer was, "Yes! Get the flight tickets booked." Crystal was very excited. She thanked me and then allowed me to go back to sleep.

I awoke several hours later with the phone on my chest and a hangover. Strangely distorted thoughts of a dream about being invited to Brunei or some far away place to perform for royalty filled my head. The dream felt so real but I started to doubt the whole thing after ringing friends and family and telling them about it. They all laughed and said, "Alan, its April Fool's Day – April Fool!" I let a couple of days pass and I still had this dream on my mind, and so I decided I needed to sort my head out. After half of an hour searching my databases I found the telephone number for Crystal's mum in Manchester. I made a call and her mum confirmed that her daughter was employed by his Royal Highness, Prince Jefri Bolkiah, in Brunei, and that she worked as his personal DJ for private functions and as a companion for his young daughter, Princess Hamidah.

My heart was now pumping. If it was a dream it was a really perceptive one; after all, I could not have known the details that Crystal's mum had given me. I had no contact number in Brunei and I could not even remember the date of the party. But, importantly, I did remember giving her my address.

On the 4th April, I was once again awakened early by a courier service wanting a signature for a small package. As I opened the envelope, to my amazement, air tickets fell out and I watched this dream become a reality in front of me. There it was, clear as day, and in black and white – and a few other colours – a return ticket with Singapore Airlines, "*upper class*". I was now completely awake, my hands were shaking, and I had to read the information on the tickets three times before it had sunk in. I was going out to Brunei on the 24th April, 1992, and returning on the 27th to perform a hypnosis show for the Brunei royal family, who were then, I believe, the richest family in the world.

Really excited, I called my parents and family to tell them my good news. They were thrilled for me as this was a one-off lifetime experience and I was determined to enjoy every second. I received another call from Crystal, instructing me that I was not to tell anybody apart from my immediate family, for security reasons. When I checked my diary I was alarmed, I had taken on another booking via my agent to put on a show in Blackpool at the same time. I called the agent immediately explaining the full situation and, reluctantly, he agreed with me that his gig would have to be postponed. This was the first time in my entire career as an entertainer that I had double booked and I have not done the same since as I pride myself on my precise organisation and never disappointing people who want to come to see me.

Stage fright is not something I suffered from but the days leading up to my departure were anxious ones for me. I would walk up and down the hallway as if treading the boards backstage before a show, wondering what to expect from the Far East, and which routines would I perform that would be in keeping for a royal performance. Who would attend the show and what type of young lady would the princess turn out to be?

Departure day finally arrived. I said my goodbyes to family and friends, just like I had done so many times previously. My itinerary comprised a domestic flight from Manchester to Heathrow, Heathrow to Singapore, and then the Sultan's own airline, Royal Brunei, to my final destination.

I allowed plenty of time to get to Manchester, departing on schedule and, upon check-in with Singapore Airlines, I was very impressed by their high standards. I was presented with an invitation to the VIP lounge where airline staff bowed to my every need. I was not used to upper class at airports. Up until then, all my flights were economy. I boarded the aircraft and was offered champagne. Wonderful! I was certainly going to enjoy this one. The flight purser introduced himself and addressed me as "Mr. Alan". He informed me that if there was anything I required, all I needed to do was to ask. I had a cheesy grin from ear to ear. I just wanted to tell everyone that I, Alan Bates, was going to Brunei to perform a hypnotic show for the royal family!

It was a very long flight indeed, the longest I had ever undertaken. I was to arrive at the airport early evening so I spent my time watching several movies and drinking copious amounts of champagne and the best Scotch whisky. I started to feel the effects. Each time my glass ran dry the flight attendant was there to fill it back up again –what a life! I managed to get a little sleep and before I knew it we were on our final approach into Lapangan Terbang Antarabangsa airport, Brunei. I was instructed not to tell anybody my business in Brunei, not even the customs or immigration officials, should I be questioned. I was rather concerned by this as, if I were to get asked, what on earth would I say?

I checked through immigration without a hitch but at the carousel I waited for my baggage and, to my disappointment, it wasn't there. I was now the only passenger left standing at the carousel with several customs officers watching me. I was now concerned and nervous. I approached them and explained about my missing suitcase and a tall officer in an immaculate uniform asked me about the one case that had been revolving for the last ten minutes. I turned and looked and, to my horror, it was my case, and it had been there all the time! I was instructed to open it and I thought that's it, what on earth do I say now? How am I going to explain away my stage props consisting of a six foot long plastic boa constrictor snake, spiders, skull and other strange stage props? The officer was not perturbed and beckoned me through.

The small airport was now completely devoid of passengers and, fortunately, I cleared customs without a further hitch. I towed my suitcase on its rear wheels out of the terminal building and to my further horror there was not one person outside, not a single car or even a taxi. I waited for a further ten minutes in complete darkness in a high temperature – no streetlights, no contact telephone number. Just silence.

I became rather concerned, I did not know who was to meet me or where I was to stay, and considering I was instructed to keep quiet about my purpose of visitation, I really didn't know what on earth to do! I was jet lagged, tired and still half drunk on the complimentary delights when I decided to return back into the terminal building and get someone to call me a taxi.

I was further shocked to learn that at sunset, the small taxi service closed for business. I was in such a pickle when an airport official offered to call the Sheraton hotel and order the courtesy car to come and pick me up. I was very disappointed as nobody had even bothered to meet me. I then decided that I would stay at any hotel and they could find me whenever – and foot the bill!

I arrived at the Sheraton Utama Hotel in Bandar Seri Begawan and to my total surprise I already had a reservation, and several messages were awaiting me from Crystal. The instructions were to freshen up (sober up!) and meet for dinner at nine-thirty. The hotel was of good standard and later I was to discover that the Brunei people were generally extremely humble, sincere, honest and very friendly. Apart from their mother language, Malay, they also all spoke very good English. I made my dinner appointment on time and was greeted by Crystal with a big friendly hug. We had a lot of catching up to do and I had many, many questions to be answered. Crystal had come a long way from a well-known nightclub DJ in Manchester to become royal servant and friend to the richest family on the planet!

Over dinner we came up to speed and all the rules were spelled out to me. I was to meet Princess Hamidah the following day. A party was being thrown to celebrate her birthday in the princess's own nightclub, with one exception: no alcohol. This was the rule of the whole, strictly Muslim, country. It was explained that the nightclub was built exactly to western standards with all the very latest equipment, and musically they were up to date though only a few kids attended her club.

It didn't take long for me to realise that ninety-five percent of the hotel patrons were on the Sultan's payroll. This was big business and when you are dealing with the richest family in the world, that big contract could make you very wealthy. I met a vast array of characters during my short stay, including many salesmen tendering for contracts that ranged from helicopters to gold bath taps, all hoping to succeed with their business.

I retired to bed with my head filled with our dinner conversation, jet lagged and still buzzing from the whole experience. I was to be picked up early in the morning and driven to meet Princess Hamidah and so I needed to have all my wits about me. I was determined to enjoy every second of this royal experience in Brunei, my only regret is that I forgot to take a camera with me. Daybreak arrived and, after a hearty breakfast, Crystal came to meet me to escort me to the palace. In Brunei royal circles, all the palaces are referred to in "house numbers".

As we approached a sentry box, I was informed that the royal family were protected by their own army which was a detachment of British-trained Ghurkhas. Crystal, with her long blond hair and blue eyes, stood out a mile. She was a well-known face and was waved on through the casual checkpoint. My adrenaline was pumping now. I was just minutes away from meeting a *real princess*. To calm me down, Crystal said, "Chill out, Alan, Princess Hamidah is really looking forward to meeting you as well." We were now in the royal grounds. We drove past two long buildings on split-levels, which were Prince Jefri's garages, and my eyes popped out of my head when I saw the contents! Crystal informed me that I could enjoy a guided tour around the garages later – first we were to meet Princess Hamidah.

As we pulled up in the courtyard, we parked next to a brand new yellow Ferrari. I noticed a little electric golf buggy making its way up to join us. Crystal said, "Here she is. This is the princess and you're here to entertain her." Wow, that was a good way to put it. I was not sure how I was going to play this one. Should I be calm and shy? Or do I act myself and be outgoing and friendly? I quickly decided to be my cheeky self. Princess Hamidah pulled up alongside our car and, accompanying her, was her cousin Citi.

The princess shyly got out of her buggy and came over to meet us. Crystal introduced me and with a nice smile I thanked her for inviting me to Brunei. The princess in turn introduced me to her cousin, who was of a similar age. I could see both girls were interested in me, purely for the reason they did not get to meet boys – certainly not cheeky English ones with fair hair and blue eyes. I now felt so much at ease. Apart from her royal status, Hamidah was just a young pretty girl who wanted to know as much about me as I did her. We hit it off as the afternoon progressed and the princess asked, "Would you like to see our polo horses?" I replied, "Sure thing," and we drove around to the stables. Prince Jefri retained a full Argentinean polo team for whenever he felt in the mood.

The Princess then asked if I would like a ride. I replied, "I would love to." One of the Argentinean stablemen beckoned me to a horse, which I mounted without fear. My younger days spent on a local farm in my home town would now come in handy. These horses were the best that money could buy. Once the princess had mounted, we were off. We did a circuit of the stables and then it was back to the group. The princess had a bodyguard who was present most of the time. He seemed to slip in and out of thin air and kept himself very much to himself. Looking back now, he was not the type of man you would want to get on the wrong side of

– "special forces", for sure. Once we finished riding, the princess was much more relaxed in my company and I suggested we go to the club where I was to perform the following day, so that I could get a feel for the place. We made our way to the venue and, after closer examination, I was very surprised to find the club better equipped than most of the UK nightclubs in which I had worked as a professional DJ.

I was now starting to see the power and wealth of this family. Cheekily, I asked Princess Hamidah what birthday gifts she had received and she casually pulled down the neck of her sweatshirt and revealed a most beautiful diamond necklace. Then she tugged at her ears to highlight her matching earrings. I was told later that the set was bought in London for over one million pounds. I was then cheeky enough again to ask what else she had received and she took me by my arm to the courtyard and pointed to the bright yellow Ferrari, next to which we had parked earlier. We got into the car, the princess in the driving seat, but she did not know how to drive, and the crazy thing, is her feet would not reach the peddles.

The princess then told me it was to add to her colour collection of Ferraris! As the afternoon progressed, I was becoming fed up addressing her as "Princess Hamidah". It seemed long and drawn out, and whilst we were in mid-conversation, I felt brave –and cheeky enough – to ask. I said quickly, "Do you mind if I call you 'Hamidah'." She replied, "I don't mind," so from then on we were on first-name terms.

The sun had started to set and it was time for us to leave the palace. Crystal asked if I would like to visit the world famous Water Village, the largest in the world, and watch the sunset. I was very keen to see as much of this lovely country as I possibly could in the short time available. The Water Village is a whole village built above the water line, supported by timber posts and built entirely of wood, with creaky passageways as the infrastructure.

We walked out onto the village and all the homes were open to see – little children were being bathed and put to bed, families preparing food. The residents were extremely friendly and I made a special effort to wave to all the kids and parents alike. The homes were very clean and tidy and I remember thinking at the time what a wonderful way of life – zero crime, no stress, and no major competition. Just a great and simple community spirit. Crystal told me that the Sultan had offered to build a whole new village on land but the residents refused as this had been their way of life for generations. The rumour was that when the Sultan married, he bought a television set for everybody that wanted one, so they could all watch the ceremony live. At this time, I would never have dreamed that one day I would be the first hypnotist on TV there and my show would be broadcast live from Kuala Lumpur throughout the whole region.

We arrived back at the hotel after a very fulfilling day and with just enough time to shower and dress for dinner. I was told that the British, American, Australian and European employees were told of my arrival and all wanted to dine with us. At the time, after sunset, everything stopped in Brunei. There are no cafés, restaurants, clubs or streetlights that I knew about, and it gets very dark. Upon arriving at the hotel restaurant, I was greeted by about 25 people. We sat around several tables and ordered local cuisine. It was such a shame there was no wine or alcohol to complement our excellent feast, only soft drinks. Our dinner conversation covered many topics, mainly my purpose of visit, the subject of hypnotism and the other occupations of my dinner guests. It turned out that all our guests were on the payroll of the royal family. The occupations varied from teachers, gym fitness trainers, personal aids and cruise ship staff.

The Sultan, owned a large yacht, which was on permanent standby for his immediate boarding, if required. While anchored out at sea, the staff came ashore to relieve their boredom. An Australian girl who worked on board told me that the boat had not moved in six months and everybody was on full pay!

After a superb dinner and charming company, it was time to retire. The following day was going to be stressful enough and I was going to need all the rest I could get. Arrangements were made to have dinner again and, possibly, a party (with some smuggled alcohol) the next evening. As we requested the bill, everybody wanted to sign the cheque and a quarrel started as to who would. Crystal told me afterwards that everyone was on an unlimited expense account and it really didn't matter who signed.

The next morning I was up bright as a button. The weather in Brunei was superb and I managed to get in a little sunbathing at the pool. I noticed a party of girls gathering around, all dressed in official uniform. When they spotted me, they came over and asked for a group photograph. I agreed, but to this day I don't know why, as they certainly didn't know me or my purpose of visit. Crystal drove over to the hotel to take me back to the palace and on the way we discussed the running procedure for the show. Crystal was going to play the music for the show and then the bombshell was dropped – among the invited guests were the Sultan's wives, Her Majesty Raja Isteri Pengiran Anak Saleha and Her Royal Highness Pengiran Isteri Hajjah Mariam, and Princes Bahar and Hakim, Hamidah's brothers.

My pre-show nerves had now really set in. I was not allowed to hypnotise any of the royal family and the total of guests invited was forty. I knew I was going to have my work cut out. What made it worse was that several of the guests' grasp of the English language was not that good.

We did the necessary sound checks and then I found myself at a table where I waited for my call time. I needed to use the toilet and I asked a royal servant where the toilets where. She pointed them out – which all seemed fine until I got there – and out of the two available doors there were no markings to identify the boys' from the girls'. Now, I have mentioned that usually I have a big chunk of good luck in my life, and so, despite being in a foreign place and surrounded with dignitaries – and on my very, very best behaviour – I crossed my fingers and took a chance, pushing hard on the right hand door.

As I burst in, I heard a loud, girly gasp of shock and surprise, catching a glimpse of a lady swathed in silks. I quickly backed out, bottom first, mumbling apologies, eyes tightly shut. I may even have bowed, I can't remember.

Yes, lady luck had for once let me down and I had blundered unwittingly into the wrong toilet. I was so embarrassed. I walked back to my seat, holding my head in my hands, repeating, "Gosh, what have I done!" I had no idea who she was but as it was thankfully never, ever mentioned, they must have seen the funny side of my predicament.

Showtime was set for two in the afternoon; I was all set and most of the guests had arrived. Sound checks were completed and props were in place. The guests gathered around the stage area, lights went down and my intro set the atmosphere, "Since the beginning of time, man has underestimated the power of the subconscious mind. Throughout human creation, certain people are born with special powers, and what you are about to see is live and unrehearsed. Allow yourself to relax, focus, and interact, for it is now time to welcome, live on stage, the true master of hypnosis, Mr. Alan Bates."

That was my cue. I made my entrance and my next words will stay with me for the rest of my life, it was a big point in my career. "You're Royal Highnesses, Princess Pengearan Anak Hamidah, ladies and gentleman, good afternoon!" I held the audience for the whole one-hour show, but I did struggle first of all in getting willing volunteers, and then when I did get six people on stage, three did not understand what I was saying and most of the audience did not know what I was doing. I ended up with three people hypnotised and, to my standards, I considered it a poor show. The royal family really did not have a clue what it was all about but I pulled it off and everybody was happy. I then retired to the dressing room, got changed and went off in search of a late lunch. I followed my nose to a massive lunch presentation "fit for a king" – and queen, and a humble hypnotist!

I met up with Crystal and we had a de-brief on the show, ate lunch and discussed life in royal circles. Hamidah could have anything she wished for. She looked through designer catalogues and one of her seven nannies ordered everything in the catalogue. When the clothing arrived it was all in the wrong size. After apologising, the nanny offered to repack and send it back when Hamidah interrupted and said, "Don't bother. Just reorder in my size." Hamidah decided she wanted to learn how to dance so she hired a professional American dance team to stay in Brunei on a retainer so whenever her mood took her she would work out with the team.

Prince Jefri, I heard, was a real character and, I suppose, a real old-time playboy. He led an exorbitantly lavish lifestyle, until his assets were frozen and many of his possessions sold off. In fact, the media had reported he had probably gone through more cash than any other human being on earth. There were rumours that, at one point, he was spending $50 million a month. I was told many stories about him but I did not get to meet him and it was not my experience. I was invited as a guest of the royal family and they treated me very well, and we should speak as we actually find. I do not believe we should betray anyone's trust lightly.

When I returned to England I was offered a sum of several thousand pounds for my story by a journalist who wrote for a national daily tabloid. The money would have been nice but my moral compass would not allow me to tell. Since my visit to Brunei, many stories have leaked to the press about Prince Jefri's parties and activities, including a former Miss America beauty queen who started litigation in a U.S. court claiming she had been invited over as a hostess but what was really wanted of her was sex.

I decided now my work was over it was time to have a tour of Prince Jefri's royal garage. Crystal took me down in her car and the only way I can explain it is – seeing is believing! The two garages ran side by side on two split-levels. Every model of Porsche lined the way, in every colour, followed by Ferrari in every colour, then on to Rolls Royce, Aston Martin, Mercedes, and every other make of prestige limited editions. Every vehicle was installed with a car phone and several mechanics were on duty to service and clean the machines. Apart from cars, there were top of the range motorbikes and tour buses with black glass windows. It was a fantastic experience alone just to see the garages and its contents.

Crystal suggested we go back to the palace and spend what little time we had left with Hamidah, as we were unsure if I would be invited back. Hamidah had a nice birthday. She was now fifteen and growing up quickly. We spent a further two hours walking and talking. She was inquisitive about life in England just as much as I was with life in Brunei.

It was time to say our goodbyes and in keeping with their tradition it is custom to give all guests a present. Rumours were going around that everybody was to receive a Rolex watch, but this was incorrect. Everybody queued up in turn to greet and wish the princess a happy birthday and one of the royal aides on her behalf presented us all with a beautifully wrapped box.

When my turn came, I wished her again happy birthday and thanked her for my invitation. I also asked her if I could use, "By Royal Appointment", on my stationary at home and she agreed.

Crystal and I made our way back to the car and, looking back over my shoulder as we left the royal grounds, I had to pinch myself to see if I had been dreaming. I was a very lucky man having experienced what I had. I was like a child at Christmas, opening my present. My gift? Well, that will remain my secret.

We made our way back to the hotel and Crystal arranged to meet our dinner guests from the previous night at 8.30 p.m. I managed to rest a while and take on board the day's events with a proud chuckle on my face. I made my way to the restaurant at our arranged time and I was informed that, after dinner, one of the guests had several bottles of vodka in his room and had invited everybody back. He also wanted me to hypnotise him. During dinner, a Ghurkha armed soldier came over to our table and requested a word with Crystal. We were concerned at what was happening when she came back to the table and said he had been instructed by Princess Hamidah to escort Mr. Bates back to the royal palace as her Royal Highness wanted to see him!" Crystal told him that I was feeling unwell and would not be able to go and he left. I will never know what she wanted that night, but after dinner we went to the party as arranged and enjoyed several vodkas. I also hypnotised two people at the party and gave everybody an entertaining time.

Once again, "all good things must come to an end". My time was up in Brunei and Crystal was going to take me back to the airport. I had just finished packing when I heard a knocking at my door. To my surprise, it was Princess Hamidah's bodyguard. I invited him in and he gave me an envelope. "The Princess would like you to have this," he explained. I thanked him and he left my room without a further word. I opened the large envelope and was delighted with its crisp sterling contents. The day was the 27th April, 1992. It was time for me to leave the kingdom and travel to my home kingdom, England.

The trip home was also an interesting experience. My connecting flight from Singapore to London gave me a six hour layover so I decided, along with a famous tennis champion that I met on the flight, to clear customs and head into the city. It was a wise decision. I found Singapore to be a fantastic place. We visited the famous Raffles Hotel, Orchard Road and several other attractions, and in no time we had to head back to the airport for our connection to London, unknown to me at the time that I would make lots of trips to Singapore in the future and perform at many venues, including the famous *"Tanglin Club"*, building a fan base, and make many good friends on the way.

It was now all over and I had the richest experience one could ever have.

Alan Bates, "By Royal Appointment".

Postscript:

Several years later, while marketing my show in the UK, I received a letter from the Lord Chamberlain's Office at Buckingham Palace, in London, that read,

Dear Mr Bates,

I am in receipt of a letter, which you sent to the "Event Organiser". While it is kind of you to write and offer your services, I was a little surprised by the words "by Royal Appointment" at the bottom of your writing paper as well on your enclosed photograph. Certain companies who hold a

Tradesman's Warrant for providing goods or services directly to a member of the Royal Family are permitted to use a similar form of words on their notepaper and certain other items. You do not hold such a warrant, and I therefore wonder by what authority you are using these words. I am afraid that unless you have documentary evidence to support this, you would have to remove these words from future material so that you do not mislead members of the public, who might otherwise think that you hold a Tradesman's Warrant.

Yours sincerely,

Jonathon Spencer.
Secretary Lord Chamberlain's Office.

I was fuming when I read the letter and promptly wrote back explaining my circumstances and connection with the Brunei Royal family. The very next day I received another letter from Buckingham Palace from the secretary of the Lord Chamberlain's Office that read as follows,

Dear Mr Bates,

Thank you for your letter dated the 25th October, and for explaining your connection with the Royal Family of Brunei. I am grateful to you for taking the trouble to do this, and for replying to my letter so promptly.

Signed yours sincerely,

Jonathon Spencer.
Secretary Lord Chamberlain's Office.

CHAPTER SIX
THE PARANORMAL EXPERIENCE

I received a telephone call late one evening in the spring of 1997 from Derek Acorah, the spirit medium. Derek sounded very excited and informed me that his spirit guide, "Sam", had told him that we were going to work the stage together and that we were going to be very successful. I had visited Derek on a couple of occasions as a paying client, and the readings and advice which I received had been extremely accurate. Derek was so excited on the phone and when he suggested we meet to discuss the idea, I instantly accepted. I tried a few scenes in my head to work out how a medium and hypnotist could successfully work together and came up with none, but I thought it would do no harm in meeting for lunch.

A few days later we met in a pleasant little Spanish restaurant in Victoria Street, Liverpool. A very excited Derek and I discussed all aspects of our respective skills and how much we each liked to interact with our audiences to give them a positive "experience" of the paranormal. We both decided that we could certainly combine our talents meaningfully and so should begin together to hire local venues to undertake the promotion and marketing. And, so, the concept was developed and "The Paranormal Experience" was born.

The Paranormal Experience is a fusion of past life regression and spiritual mediumship, demonstrated to a very high standard. The show is split into two segments; firstly, the past life regression is demonstrated by myself, with willing volunteers allowing me to hypnotise them into a very deep trance state, and by accepting the psychological key, they journey back in time into a past life. This is all done live on stage to an audience of hundreds. After an informative talk on regression, I invite twenty participants on stage and, once I complete my induction, I start the journey back in time. Each show still fascinates me; they are so unpredictable. Very often, the subjects change sex and persona, will speak in totally different voices, and, on rare occasions, will even speak in different languages. I stress that none of this is contrived in any way and that these people are audience members and, as such, are unknown to me.

Once I have made contact in a past life, I interview and record the information that I receive and, at the end of the demonstration, I read back to them their past life history. The information that I receive is later given to the volunteers and may be researched if they choose to do so. I will provide you with samples of regressions later in this chapter. In all of our demonstrations, I choose a regression case of interest and I place a time datum marker in their subconscious mind, allowing me to return back to this incarnation and time period later in the show.

After an interval break, the second segment is conducted by Derek. Derek, who really is a very gifted medium, enters the stage and uses his gift to contact departed spirits of the loved ones in the audience. Messages that often prove, without any shadow of a doubt, the existence of life after death, are then gently passed to recipients. Derek does this in a most sensitive manner, as when this is experienced "live" it has a powerful effect on people and can completely amaze theatre audiences.

At the end of Derek's presentation, he then welcomes me back to the stage and we invite the chosen regression case from earlier in my demonstration to join us. I then regress the subject back to the time datum that I installed earlier. What happens next is extremely specialised; Derek proceeds to link into the past life incarnation and communicate with the spirit of a person that lived sometimes hundreds of years ago. All this is recorded for the individuals for future research.

So What is Past Life Regression?

This is a question I frequently get asked and I usually answer by giving the following information. To my mind, we have four possible descriptions of what is happening.

1/. Past life regression is a genuine psychic phenomenon, where contact is assisted by an induced hypnotic state that links to some historically lived experience, which may be documented and able to be checked and verified.

2/. Past life regression is a manipulation of the imagination and fantasy, like a sort of controlled dream. As in a detailed and lucid experience of unconscious material, a story is weaved that is unrelated to any historic, and therefore real characters, who ever lived. Such information, of course, would be unverifiable, no matter how true they sounded.

3/. Past life regression is a direct experience of genetically inherited information. For example, someone might perhaps be seeing vivid images from an *ancestor's* life – say, a great grandfather's memories of the First World War.

4/. Past life regression is utter nonsense.

Throughout history, mankind has sought answers to the many mysteries of life. Since the dawn of time – and many years before Christianity – people have believed in life after physical death. But it has always been just that – a belief – and an act of faith, without any scientifically accepted proof. The sceptics, atheists, materialists – call them what you will – have always decried the evidence.

Many religious movements – Buddhist, Hindu, and some Greek philosophers – teach that reincarnation is the way that we, as human souls, develop merit. Our spirits pass from one incarnation on the earth plane to heaven / hell / nirvana, or whatever other name one may give to the appointed place for some form of judgement. Souls then achieve this state permanently, unless lacking in some way – or if the soul actually chooses to return – wherein the soul reincarnates back into the world.

In other words, we have our entrances and our exits, and one soul, in its time, must play many parts. We are, then, unconsciously, the sum of all those previous parts, yet within our individual psyche exists the memory of all our eternal life.

My method of unlocking the secrets of our past lives lies within the mystery of using the hypnotic trance to deepen people's ability to focus. The subjects are placed in a hypnotic state and then proceed to travel back in time to a past life. In this deeply relaxed state they can link to and relive the parts they played while incarnated in a different body, in a different time and place.

Many of us have experienced the near reality of a memory, indelibly imprinted on our minds, as we conjure up almost forgotten images from some important event in our lives. So it is with the regressed subjects - back they go, beyond the first memories of childhood, deeper and deeper they travel, passing the point of birth, conception and on into the mysteries of their previous life.

Witnessing a professional hypnotist working with a good subject may change your understanding of life as we comprehend it. As I mentioned, with Derek's material, this can feel disturbing when witnessed live. Past life regression offers an insight into the true nature of our own soul's eternal existence. The barriers to the subject's hidden incarnations dissolve as the regression leads them back beyond the veil of birth.

Right from the initial steps, the stage demonstration bookings were coming in fast and furious and we were regularly packing out venues in the North West of England. And so it was not long before the TV producers got to know what we were doing. Derek was still providing private consultations, and he gave readings for several of the production staff at Granada TV. They were so impressed that they offered Derek his own show on the Granada Breeze channel – the start of his TV career. By working very hard, he justly received the status of the most popular spirit medium in the country. Soon, the first of his many books was published, entitled, *The Psychic World of Derek Acorah*. On 16th January,

1999, Derek and I dissolved the theatrical partnership, though we both still felt at the time that our combined show had plenty of life in it. And, indeed, several years later, it did return and would go from strength to strength.

Exorcism

Before we embarked on our solo careers, Derek often received calls from people who claimed they where being haunted, and we were often asked if we could help. We called it "Ghost Busting", and every so often he would ring up and say, "Alan, another ghost busting job has cropped up. Do you want to come?" I was always there in a flash. I was now mentally strong enough to handle paranormal activity. Gone were the times when I could not move around in my old thatched cottage after dark. We successfully exorcised several homes and business premises using a technique Derek had mastered over time to rid spirits – good and evil – from both places and times in which they didn't belong.

One particular exorcism has stayed in my mind. The mother of a sixteen-year-old boy from Liverpool contacted Derek claiming a spirit was wrecking her family, her young son near to having a nervous breakdown. In cases like this, it didn't matter how busy our schedules were, we dropped everything and went to their assistance. It was interesting how the story unfolded.

Upon arriving at the very pleasant, semi-detached family home, Derek immediately detected the presence of a spirit. We sat around a table in the lounge, drinking tea with the mother of the family, her two daughters and young son, who all looked pale and totally drained. None of them made a peep as the mother explained her story. For several weeks, her son claimed to have been woken up many times during the night by the duvet cover being dragged off him in bed.

The poor lad didn't understand what was happening, but it evolved into a more serious problem when one particular night, as the cover had been pulled down, he felt hands around his neck and started to choke. Just as he was about to pass out, the hands

106

let go, and he screamed for help. His mother woke up and rushed into his room to find her son trembling and in a very distressed state. His younger sister had also witnessed this grim presence in his bedroom.

We asked the boy to take us alone up to his room, so we could have his version of events, and during his explanation he broke down and wept. Our hearts went out to him; he was a nice young man and clearly had a genuine problem. I then escorted him downstairs to sit with his mum and sisters, and re-joined Derek in the boy's bedroom. As soon as I went back in the room I could feel it. Derek had his eyes closed and, in silence, focused on the energy in the room. The temperature had dropped dramatically and I could readily sense a strong presence. After several minutes, he said, "Alan, I am now getting a clear picture of what has happened here. We must go downstairs and again talk to the family."

Derek explained to all of us that the boy's father had witnessed a motorbike crash in the nearby country lanes and had rushed to the man's aid. The family nodded their heads in agreement. The motorcyclist had died in their father's arms and, upon returning home, the confused spirit had attached himself to their father and then resided in the family home. He explained that the spirit was not evil but had not passed over fully, and so was expressing his anger and confusion. This was being picked up by the young boy who was very sensitive and "open".

Then came the twist in the story. Derek astonished us all by saying he had contacted the boy's father, who had recently died of a heart attack, and passed on from him messages of love. The expressions on the family's faces were a picture; they had not mentioned anything about their father's recent passing, and certainly nothing about the motorcycle accident. Derek had once again proved his genuine "gift". He informed the family that we were next going to go back to the room where he would attempt to get the spirit to leave.

We set the room ready for the "candle rite," laid out the crystals and flowers, and Derek asked me to assist by focusing on peace and sending out thoughts for the spirit, while he made contact. After about twenty minutes of silence, the atmosphere in the room changed dramatically. It felt like a heavy burden had been removed from my shoulders and the room became serene and peaceful. He further explained that the spirit had not accepted the fact that he had died in the accident; he was confused and had become very frustrated because nobody would listen nor pay any attention to him. That was why he vented his anger on the boy, because he was open to the spirit world and could sense his presence.

During the candle rite, a departed female family member of the motorcyclist appeared before Derek and assured him and the spirit it was time for the cross over, and the relative was there to guide him. The spirit departed, and we were left both emotionally drained. We went downstairs with the family for a final cup of hot tea and assured them that they would not have any more problems.

Each time we conducted an exorcism, it was a very rewarding experience. I would never have even believed I would witness one in all my life, never mind be involved in a small way.

So, after going our different ways, for a few years, Derek and I joined forces again, and this time – armed with more knowledge and a lot more experience – the "Paranormal Experience" was back in the theatres, and ready this time to tour the United Kingdom. Times are far and few when people meet and are allowed to exercise their separate and special talents together. What we had was unique, different, and a breath of fresh air in psychic circles. The stories I'm now going to present are from live shows – and they will take your breath away.

With all my experience of past life regression, I have only made contact with two famous people. You may think that I would encounter lots of famous historical personalities, but this is certainly not the case. The first case was during a show that Derek and I were presenting at Fort Regent, in St. Helier, on 30th October, 2010, on the beautiful island of Jersey, in the Channel Islands. One of the volunteers was regressed back in time to apparently being a well-known opera singer in Paris. Sadly, I do not have the information on the regression as a copy was not made when the recording was presented to the participant. The second case – "regression two" – below, is of a more sinister nature, and the very subject is still drawing world fascination. So, read on!

Author & Derek Acorah, theatre dressing room

Regression One

On 22nd March, 2011, Derek and I were performing at the Garrick Playhouse Theatre, near Manchester, when I experienced one of the most amazing emotional regressions that I have ever witnessed. We were performing to a full house, the audience all eagerly waiting and ready to participate. Shortly after we had made our joint stage entrances and been introduced, Derek retired from the stage and I commenced my induction. Nothing could have prepared me for what we were about to tap into.

I had twenty willing participants on stage and nine of them were successfully regressed into past lives, all living in long forgotten times – and then I made contact in a past life with a lady named Joyce Ashton.

Joyce was deeply regressed to the Second World War and was living in Dewsbury, a small town near Leeds, with her husband, Thomas, and their young son, Robert. Thomas Ashton was a British soldier, an engineer, and held the rank of private. Thomas was killed in enemy action in Belgium on 2nd October, 1941, but his body was never recovered.

Meanwhile, Joyce was raising Robert singlehandedly, contributing to the war effort by making tank shells in a munitions factory, named Steeton's. Steeton's, it seems, was a really big factory and people were bussed in from a 20 miles radius to work there. Lots of day to day information was recorded about her life in general, including St. Johns School and Anglican Church, which her son Robert attended. The feeling that I was receiving from Joyce was one of deep sadness, due to the loss of her husband. By now, the entire theatre audience were sitting on the end of their seats, listening in complete silence, and you could have cut the atmosphere with a knife.

I then progressed with the timeline of this regression incarnation to Joyce's eventual passing. I guided her to the last moments of that life, and she relived it for us, sharp with tears and sadness. Joyce gave an accurate account of how she worked and how to pack down the explosive charge on a press. There was an accident – a shell exploded and killed four people, including Joyce. Joyce was working on the press with three other women when a spark ignited the gunpowder and blew the press to pieces, killing all of the women. When I asked what her last thoughts were, she replied with tears rolling down her cheeks: "Who is going to look after my child now?" The audience gasped with emotion, such was the atmosphere in the theatre. After the regression had ended, I brought Joyce forward to the present time, and by now she was fully aware that some powerful emotion had moved her deeply due to the fact that her eye mascara and makeup, mixed with her tears, had run into her lap.

The regression subject was a lady named Gillian Perry, from Manchester. Gillian is a calm, intelligent and down-to-earth person, who has never been to Dewsbury and was unaware of the entire event.

Postscript:

Research was conducted into the information that we had received during the regression and it transpired that Steeton's ammunition factory did exist, but sadly all that is left now is just a small square red brick building, named the pill box, and, surprisingly, it is a "listed building". We could not find any records for this particular accident, but a lot of accidents were hushed up for morale and propaganda purposes and, at most, received an inch or two in the local paper, with no mention of exactly where the people died, other than "a factory".

St. Johns School and Anglican Church, which her son Robert attended, exists in Dewsbury. There are registered births and deaths for Joyce and her husband, a birth entry for her son, but not a death certificate. Could you imagine the consequences if a search for her son was successful and what it would be like to re-unite them today? There is the possibility that he may still be alive. Maybe he was evacuated to Australia or Canada and adopted after the war – a lot of maybes, I know - but maybe his mother still needs to know he has had a good life. We may never know, but one thing is sure, Gillian had an amazing past life regression and a life deepening experience.

The jewel in the crown in our research was the discovery of T. W. Ashton on the war memorial in Crow's Nest Park, Dewsbury.

Regression Two

On 7th September, 2006, I was presenting a show at the Haydock Cricket Club in Lancashire. This particular show was before Derek and I had returned with The Paranormal Experience. This evening, the audience members were very excited. One could feel the atmosphere upon entering the auditorium and I was very keen to start the performance.

As usual I had twenty volunteers on stage and I was happy with my delivery and presentation, and, of course, the quality of the regressions, being most important. Halfway through the show, I regressed a middle-aged, well-spoken lady into a very deep trance state, and while communicating with her in a past life, it transpired she lived in London, and her name was Mary Kelly. The year was circa 1888 and her regressed incarnation was a working prostitute. All aspects of her private and working life unfolded on my stage, including Mary providing sexual services to seamen, and when I mentioned different nationalities, including the French, she remarked that she had worked a brothel in Paris. Mary also added that she had an illegitimate child. She said that times were very hard and she was leading a very sad life.

As the dialogue continued, and the information continued to flow, I guided her to the final part of her incarnation, and she started to tell me that she was brutally murdered. At this point, a man in the audience stood up and shouted loudly, "Mary Kelly was the last prostitute to be murdered by Jack the Ripper!" I did not know this, but now the audience were buzzing with excitement. At the end of the session, once the regression subjects were returned to "local time", I proceeded to interview this lady, live on stage. She had no memory of what had happened, to where she had travelled, nor to who she once had been. I was teasing her over the microphone, to the delight of the audience, when I said, "Would you like to know what work you did in London in 1888? This rather reserved lady was curious as to why the whole audience and I were focusing on this particular point. She said, "Yes. Please tell me." And, after a little more teasing and milking her curiosity, I said, "You were a prostitute. And, it gets worse – you were murdered by Jack the Ripper!" The expression on her face was priceless. You could see she was genuinely taken aback, speechless. I used my charm and cheeky demeanour to best effect and reassured her that this was in the past and bore no reference on her present life.

Postscript:

After the show, I was so excited to get home to research information on Mary Kelly. I was thrilled to bits as everything she said during the regression was very accurate. She also gave us additional information that is not in the public domain. Looking back, I believe I sadly missed the opportunity to ask her the most important question – the identity of Jack the Ripper. If I had done so, we may have had the identity and the answer to an age old mystery.

Regression Three

In 2008, The Paranormal Experience tour was booked into the Gladstone theatre, near my former home in the lovely "garden village" of Port Sunlight. The theatre sits beautifully within the *olde worlde* heritage village that was built by Lord Leverhulme, the founder of the world famous Sunlight Soap Empire. He built the village at the turn of the century for his workers as a deliberate attempt to create a village full of the valuable social amenities for a healthy and happy life, for all his workers. There are allotments, churches, a hospital, a swimming pool, village greens and a charming museum, all beautifully integrated into the site. It is an absolute "must visit" place, especially in the summer.

Derek and I had performed at the theatre there in the past. But, on this occasion, one particular regression case stood out from the rest and is worthy of inclusion in this chapter. This regression was so filled with emotion and with such a great amount of clear detail that, after the demonstration, Derek and I decided to research and film the results.

It was here that I met Mr. Mike Boyd, a care worker from Wallasey. I regressed him back through the passage of time to 11th November, 1735, in the city of Gloucester, England. His name in this past life was Jack Mahon. Jack was 18 years of age, and from first contact, he spoke with a completely different dialect, in keeping with folk from that part of England, yet very different from his usual voice. Jack worked for a company named H. & Sons and lived in a house on Skinner Street in the city. There were no numbers on the houses there and his house was described only by the colour of its door. Derek interacted well with Jack throughout the regression and the following further information was received.

Jack had taken a fancy to a young lady named Mary Jane Smith and, at the age of twenty, they married and had one son, John, named after his grandfather. At the age of four, John had had a walking difficulty which was never rectified. They were a religious family and attended the local Church of England church. Jack had no official

H & Sons, circa 1850

schooling but received some education as a child at the church and from two people he called Father James and Sister Anne. Throughout the regression, Jack's playful character became very obvious. Sister Anne did not like frogs and during one Sunday service he placed a frog onto the pew next to her. The result was exactly what Jack had anticipated – screams and uproar. At certain times, for reasons we didn't discover in the dialogue, Jack was punished by *birching* – sometimes known as whipping or flogging. This punishment was widely used at that period in history, and it was still being used in the Isle of Man up until January 1976, when I was a child. People on the mainland kept writing to the papers about how effective it was to thrash kids with "the birch" and asking for it to be brought back!

Information regarding his work at H. & Sons revealed discrepancies with their accounts, and Jack's position within the company was what would be described today as a stock taker. Jack had discovered that commodities on the docks were not tallying with inventories and this led, as it usually does, to conflict with the workers he was associated with. Overall, I believe that Jack lived a happy life. Towards the end of the regression, I instructed him to travel within the timeline of this incarnation to his eventual passing. In his last few moments, his breathing slowed and his body calmed dramatically. During the whole regression, his hands had been shaking, but now, in these final

The Coach & Horses on Skinner Street

moments, his body began to settle, and he became very peaceful. Jack died at home while his wife Mary tended to him. Derek, who was very intensely focussed on the situation, picked up a strange fragrance – possibly of an old form of disinfectant that may have been used – and then, just at the moment of passing, he also picked up the presence of an old lady, possibly his mother in spirit form.

Jack's body was buried in his local churchyard.

Postscript:

We were in possession of so much material that a decision was made to investigate further, and so arrangements were made with Square One Pictures, under the guidance of producer Roger DaSilva and the watchful eyes of New York film director, Chase Johnston Lynch, to travel to the city of Gloucester with the subject, Mike Boyd. Some research was conducted before our travel and we discovered that the church, Skinner Street and H. & Sons had existed in the year

1735, and the business continued to trade. The picture shows H. & Sons circa 1850. It was all getting very interesting. As we entered Skinner Street on foot, Mike became rather emotional. Our research concluded that Mike's home had been demolished, but he did not know this at the time and had a *déjà vu* feeling when he stood in Skinner Street, pointing out where his house once stood. This proved

Mike Boyd, author & Derek Acorah on set

correct, too, according to the plans at the local archives.

Mike experienced a sensation of being drawn to the old abbey. Here, he pointed out that all the graves had been removed in 1800. This gave him feelings of a past soul *progression* to the present day, linking his past life to the present one. This raises the question: "Do those souls from our past lives also link in with our present soul?" Efforts to find the grave were dashed when we discovered a lot of the graves were lost and buildings had been developed on the former burial grounds.

This was really satisfying to me. In my view, this is what past life regression is all about, not just a grunt and groan, the name of a country, and the name of a husband or wife. This is the meat on the bones, verifying against all odds the proof of the spirit or soul progressing from generation to generation.

Regression Four

This is my final story of regression, so join me as we visit Liverpool, a world famous city, and rightly so, with its diverse cultures, its friendly inhabitants, great history, and, of course, The Beatles.

The date is 18th April, 2012, and I was invited by my friend, Anna Harrison, to give a private regression to one of her friends, who I will name Edward. Edward is a serving police officer in North Wales but he resides on the Wirral, just a few miles west of Liverpool, and commutes across the English - Welsh border, to and from his work. I had not met Edward before but he struck me as a nice gentleman, well mannered, of sound mind, and very professional.

Edward entered into a trance state very quickly and his communication was very clear and audible. He rapidly regressed back to a lifetime that was lived near the dockland in Liverpool, in the year 1902. His incarnate name here was John Pritchard. He gave his address as 5 Cuthbert Street, Liverpool, and he was aged 27 at the point of contact. John was married to Brenda, two years his junior, and he described himself as an abusive and violent alcoholic. His local pub was The Cross Foxes.

During his early childhood, he attended the school of St. Mary's, and although a Catholic, did not go to church or follow his religion. Money was very scarce and, looking back, the working classes had it so very much harder in those days, in comparison to what we have experienced in current times. His parents were John and Margaret. Even as a young child, he was very unhappy. There were no children born from this marriage to Brenda and, as time progressed, he became more violent and abusive to his wife. It was not a happy existence; from childhood to old age, the poverty was crippling.

John was a docker, or *stevedore*, and his job was to unload wool from the ships into boxes. Now, during the regression, I had noticed he was continually rubbing and scratching his arms. He explained that the wool constantly itched his arms and that his arms and hands were always red raw.

Then, towards the end of the regression, I guided him to the last hour of this existence. He described the scene up to his last breath, aged 68, a doctor and his wife present to hear his last words as he lay in bed at his home. His liver was shot with the ravages of alcoholism, and he felt that Brenda would surely be relieved that he had gone.

I had one more final question: "Where is your body buried?" He replied, "In a churchyard in South Allerton, Liverpool, and the headstone is near to a tree."

Postscript:

I left Edward after the session, but not before we chatted briefly on what I had experienced during the regression. He remembered nothing at all and was a little taken aback when I recapped on his past life.

I recorded the whole regression for Edward to take home with him. Since then, he has conducted his own research into the life of "John Pritchard" and has confirmed that virtually the whole regression was verifiable. However, the one thing that he cannot find is the final resting place – his grave.

Edward is a very proud Welshman, but he told me something very interesting. "Every time I travel into the city of Liverpool, I have a strange feeling of coming home."

Note: After touring for several years and regressing thousands of people, I have collected many audio recordings, and a small sample of them are available to listen to live on my regression website - www.pastlives.tv. I do hope you enjoy them.

CHAPTER SEVEN
THE SPIRIT WORLD

Many people doubt the whole idea of spirit and the spirit world. They consider what we now might call the paranormal, spirits and such, as *irrational* and *unscientific*. Others, like me, consider that these events are natural events, part of our world, that science has not yet properly focussed on, and has not even generated the tools to explore. For me, they have been a part of my life for as long as I can remember. In my experience, if you talk openly about these things, with no rigid belief system, or other axe to grind, then a lot of people will equally open up with an uncanny tale of their own to tell. And often it's the "rational" and "scientific" ones that sidle up to you quietly at the end of the show to buttonhole you with theirs.

From my very early childhood, I can recollect memories of "strange goings on", and the stories I am now going to tell are either first-hand from my own experience or from people I trust, as in close family speaking directly of their encounters. Up until my thirties I was very wary of anything that "went bump in the night", but as time has passed, my attitudes have matured to a point where now I enjoy unexplained, esoteric and other mysterious or "haunting" experiences. It would be very easy for me to write a book, never mind a chapter, on ghosts and the paranormal; however, for the purpose of this book, I am limiting the stories to only those involving my family and our experiences only.

I became very interested in psychics and mediums, and so I began to explore the whole area. Please understand that I am a "free thinker" and open to new ways of looking at things, but I do not suffer fools gladly and they all have to prove themselves beyond any reasonable doubt and to my criteria, before they even get my interest. However, I have visited many good *instruments* including Leigh Carole, Anna Harrison, Gary Dakin, Mrs. Hargreaves, Gwen Harrison, Ken Davies, "Liverpool May", Stuart Murdoch, "Southport Maria", and world famous spirit medium, Derek Acorah. Derek and I were later to set up a very successful show/demonstration, which we toured in theatres around Britain, called The Paranormal Experience, a fusion of mediumship and past life regression. This was a fascinating time for me and one which I will describe fully in a separate chapter later in the book.

Many years ago, during a private reading with the psychic, Ken Davies, from Chester, I was told that I would write a book, and it is interesting to note that shortly afterwards I was told the same by another local medium, Ian Pittman, from Wallasey. This was while taking part in a live radio programme with Radio City in Liverpool, on Halloween in 1999. After the programme ended, I asked Ian if he could pick up on any vibes from me and he said, "Alan, you are going to write a book." So that one seems to be coming true, even as I write and you read, but of course it could have been how the idea first took root. Now, not every message is accurate and not every medium is genuine, but the accurate information that I have received from some of these gifted people over many years has proved to me the existence of a positive force in nature that we really do not understand but which has fascinated mankind since the dawn of humanity.

I am not afraid of dying, and I hope the following experience that I endured will be comforting to those readers who perhaps are. In October 2006, I experienced terrible abominable pain and was admitted as an emergency case to hospital. It transpired that I had a ruptured bowel and required immediate emergency surgery. The consultant who operated on me, Mr. Ciaran Walsh, saved my life. They informed me that if I'd arrived at the hospital any later, I would have died. What he did not tell me was that, at one point during my operation, the surgical staff nearly lost me and, for some time, it was touch-and-go whether I would survive. This information was relayed back to me from one of the theatre technicians to a member of my family, and I was only told after I had made a full recovery.

During the operation, and while still under full anaesthetic, I experienced an incredibly beautiful type of "near-death experience". I felt that I had left my body behind and was given the option of passing over to "the other side" or returning to my physical body. Crazy as it now sounds, the euphoric feeling that I experienced was so deeply moving that I chose to leave the physical world and die. I can promise you that, when it's your time, there is nothing to fear in death, as it is a peaceful and pain-free experience. As it turned out, it was not my time, and after yet another "close encounter", it seemed the universe was not ready to release me!

I once met a Dutch undertaker, of all people, while filming a television show in March 2002, and I asked him, "With your personal experience of death, what are your views on dying?" He simply replied, "Death is part of living." If one looks deep into that answer, you will see that the undertaker is absolutely correct. The dying process is very much part of our living experience. We come into this world and at some point we leave. It's a balanced and completely natural event. We are, in effect, born to die.

The short stories I share below are true and accurate accounts of experiences that, over time, my family and I have witnessed. I hope you enjoy them. All our attempts to rationally explain them, to my mind, have failed.

The Man on the Stairs

My family and I were all seated for evening dinner at our early home in Town Meadow when all of a sudden all hell let loose in the hall, just outside the kitchen. It was as if several children ran together, shouting and stamping their feet, and, yet, as a family, we were alone in the house. And this was not to be the only experience of strange ghostly activity in this house. On several occasions, doors would open and close by themselves. I remember particularly one day my dad saying he had arrived home early from work and was in the bathroom, reading the newspaper, when he clearly heard the sound of what he thought was an old man climbing the stairs between floors and gasping for breath on each stair tread. Dad was the only person in the house – or so he thought – and he rushed out of the bathroom in search of the intruder. It did not take long for dad to come to the conclusion, after searching the entire house, including the loft space, that he was not the only soul in the house – except the other one didn't have a body!

Ghostly Reception

Then when we moved to our next home, a lovely cottage in Carnsdale Road, Moreton, it seemed it wasn't long before "paranormal" activity started to happen there, too. Dad was working in the kitchen on his business paperwork and, while concentrating, and at the same time listening to some relaxing music on the radio, the radio turned itself off via the volume switch. Dad thought it strange but simply switched it back on and carried on working. About a minute later, the same thing happened again, except that this time dad was consciously aware that he had watched the volume control button turn and switch itself off. I can remember dad joining us in the lounge, scratching his head, as he explained what had just happened.

Several times we have smelled the unmistakable sweet odour of pipe tobacco in the rear garden and on the patio area. This led to us reasoning that if this was the actions of a "ghost" then it was most probably a male.

Gary was lying in bed in the early hours one morning when a loud tapping on his bedroom window startled and woke him. Gary's bed was situated right next to the window and his immediate thoughts were that it was me, arriving home with no house keys. Swiftly, he pulled open the curtain, but there was nobody there. This happened several times to his annoyance.

Now, perhaps my dad – and, to some degree, Gary, John and myself – are particularly sensitive to vibrations like this, as sometimes we would all hear, smell or sense things in this house. They did not frighten us in any way, but they were *unusual*. And maybe these are not trapped souls or personalities, deliberately haunting a place, but some sort of "house memories", captured or recorded somehow by the substance of the building, or whatever, and replayed to minds, which are relaxed, aware, or open enough in that moment.

Several more "unexplained" things happened in our new home, including a banging on what felt like all the windows throughout the cottage simultaneously. In a flash, dad, Gary and I were outside the house, looking for whoever was there – but not a soul was in sight. Now, the surroundings were such that it would have been impossible to run off without being seen. This happened again on a further two occasions, but no one was ever seen.

We even had ghostly "pet" effects as, several years later, after my grandmother had passed away and we had inherited her little Shih Tzu pet dog, "Mr. Chips". When Chips died, and on several occasions, we believe he came back in ghost form, to visit my brother, John. There were often times that John could smell his distinct odour and clearly hear his little footsteps walking up and down on the tiled kitchen floor as he had done so regularly before his death.

Mr. Chips was not the only animal to haunt our home. Dad needed to use the bathroom in the early hours one morning and as he left his bedroom he saw a mysterious black cat sitting in the hallway. As he approached, the cat turned and walked into the adjacent bedroom. Dad followed and put on the light. However, to his amazement, there was no cat there – it had just disappeared!

The Dangers of the Ouija Board

In my teenage years, Gary and I, along with several friends – and probably countless others up and down the country – experimented with the Ouija board. We were at a friend's house, one night, in mid-session with a spirit contact, when a picture above my head swung to one side and, before it could drop to the floor, I was up and out of the room with lightning speed. It was impossible that anybody could have tampered with the frame as I was sat directly underneath it. What drew my attention to the frame was that I heard a noise above my head. I was now standing in-between the dining room and the lounge where our friends parents were watching television. I decided not to physically participate any further, but as the television news was broadcasting, I asked my friends to ask the spirit to predict the football results. The spirit answered immediately and when the results came on the screen a few moments later, we were all dumfounded as they were all correct!

From my experiences, I have no doubt the Ouija board does work. How and why, I don't know. But I also believe that inexperienced and tender-minded people should not meddle with it. Many years ago it was sold in toy shops as a game by the "Waddington" company, and I believe the instructions on the box read, "For children eight years and over!" A friend of mine, Andrew Dean, sadly now deceased, was the Vicar at Woodchurch Holy Cross church. He also acted as the exorcist for the Chester diocese, so anyone with complaints of haunting, demonic possession, etc., were directed to him. He told me that 98 percent of the times he was called out to people's homes, they were false alarms. For example, the older generation may mishear the beeping of smoke alarms, due to the alarm battery needing a change, and so on.

However, the remaining two percent, he was sure, were indeed "paranormal" activity. Reverend Dean also told me that on many visits he'd made to houses that were supposed to be haunted, the occupants confessed to using the Ouija board. In his opinion, "They had opened channels, and when they finished the session did not close them, and this was the reason why they were facing the consequences."

The Titanic Ghost

In chapter one, I wrote about my early adventures with Leasowe lighthouse and the old smugglers cottage in Wallasey.

The Wirral peninsular is surrounded on three sides with two wide rivers and the Irish Sea and is a natural home to sailors and tales of the sea. The strangest encounter I ever had with the Ouija board was many years later in Portland, Maine, in the United States. After telling ghost stories one evening and discussing paranormal topics with a group of friends, we decided to use the Ouija board. We contacted a spirit that communicated with us, claiming he had died on board the R.M.S. *Titanic*. At the time, my friends and I knew very little detail or history about the ship, apart from that she had sunk on her maiden voyage. The big Hollywood feature film, featuring Kate Winslet and Leonardo DiCaprio, would not be made until many years later. The spirit communicator informed us that he had died on board the ship as a result of burning to death, which we all thought was a little odd as the ship had sunk and everyone would expect death to be attributed to drowning. The spirit, moving the planchette, explained further – and in a rapid manner – that his death was caused when the water entered the boiler room and blew up the boiler that he was standing next to. He told us his name was Bessant and he was a fireman, which we all took to mean that he was literally a fireman – as in "a man who fought fires". I was to find out later that a fireman, also named a *stoker*, was a person who stoked the coal into the boilers to generate steam for the turbine engines.

When I next had the opportunity, while on a visit to London, I registered with the Kew Record Office in advance and made an appointment to view the *Titanic* passenger and crew list. The Kew Records Office holds many of the UK's historical documents and security is taken very seriously. Upon arrival I had to show my registration, appointment card and ID, and had to wait a short time for the assistant to bring over the documents that I had requested. Eventually, my name was called and I received a large brown shoebox style box and settled at an empty table where I could study. As I opened the box of memories, nothing could have prepared me for what I felt. I was overwhelmed – it was like opening Pandora's Box. I can best describe it as a box of sadness, and the historic contents made me feel dizzy. As I studied the crew list, my heart went out to the poor souls that perished that day, 15th April, 1912. In total, the ocean claimed 1,517 men, women and children. A typical example could read, "Joseph Roberts aged 15, Huyton, Liverpool bell boy missing at sea," The list seemed endless. I focused my study on the crew list, specifically the occupation of firemen / stoker and, to my utter shock and amazement, William Bessant was listed in the records!

The Masonic Ghost

While practising an ancient Masonic ritual in my lodge, in Parkgate, Wirral, in the late 1990s, my brother, Gary, and I experienced a ghostly presence in the temple. I was the senior warden of the lodge and I was occupying my rightful seat. Seated near to me was the temple inner guard, Brother Gary. At a certain point in the ceremony, the temperature dropped rapidly, and I was not alone in feeling the temperature change because Gary looked at me a little uneasily. At the same time this happened, I felt a strong presence around me, and the flame on the candle placed on my pedestal moved from vertical to forty-five degrees and remained like that for a couple of minutes. It was as if somebody or something was slowly blowing the candle flame.

Gary and I looked at each other in amazement and after the ceremony had completed we were eager to get outside and discuss the incident over dinner. After ruling out several different theories, including a draught, which would not have been possible there, how could this have happened? We concluded it must have been a presence. After making several enquiries, I learned that an elderly Masonic brother had collapsed and died in the senior warden's chair in the past.

The Great Pyramid, Egypt

As part of my birthday celebration I took a cruise on the River Nile. It was a stunning holiday and a must for advancing your historic knowledge and experience of the ancient world. However, I was to experience a very strange and unexpected sensation while queuing to enter the Great Pyramid.

My girlfriend at the time was Alnifa and she and I had joined the line of tourists eager to enter this world-famous sacred and deeply atmospheric site. As we steadily climbed into the corridor in slow formation, I felt the recognisable signs of a gathering presence. As we advanced higher, the passageway became cramped, and it was at this point that I felt the atmosphere change and became very agitated.

Alnifa, who'd experienced none of this, looked puzzled and asked me what was wrong. I replied, "Can you not feel the overwhelming sensation in this area?" It was obvious that I was the only person that had picked up on this atmosphere and by now we were well past the point of exiting the way we came in without causing a very serious disturbance to all around us, so I had to continue on with the tour. But, whatever – or whoever – the oppressing sensation was, it continued to follow me for about five minutes and then slowly disappeared, leaving only the stale air in the chamber.

Living in a Haunted Cottage

When the "Old Thatched Cottage" in Bebington, on the Wirral, came on the market, it was my dream come true. Years before, I used to drive past this beautiful old cottage and I had several dreams of one day owning it. My dreams came to fruition, but I had one problem – I was sure that I was sharing it with several other inhabitants. Inhabitants which, as my father might say, "Were not paying their share of the rent!" Several ghosts were lodging with me and eventually the atmosphere and activity became so intense that I sold the house and I moved out. But I think "the others" are probably still there.

The cottage was built circa 1653, though may have been built earlier, and for a period of time it was used as a roadside inn serving drinks to travellers commuting between Liverpool and

Chester. The local library reference states that Oliver Cromwell had stayed overnight while his horses were quartered at nearby St. Andrews church. Later on it was used as two dwellings and then even later it was turned into one home. So, I suppose, with my family's track record, I should have expected such a house to have "hidden depths".

When I purchased the property, the interior decoration had not been touched since the sixties, but after several months of hard work it became quite a comfortable home – though not without incident and some interference from my invisible lodgers. Right from the start, many of the workmen on site experienced "paranormal" – or certainly disturbing – activity, to one degree or another. Dougie, my brother's father in law, was on stepladders painting the old ship's timber beams which supported the thatched roof when several times he felt penetrating eyes piercing him while he worked.

Big Neil Jones, who was the current powerlifting world champion, sensed movement around him and was very nervy working alone in the house. Another builder, Mark, had a similar experience to my father in Town Meadow Lane when the radio he was listening to switched itself off three times! And while Billy was mixing mortar, a presence or something rushed past him, causing him to trip up. One of the bedrooms that had not been used for many years had an odd cold spot, which disappeared after renovation, and this room also made people feel dizzy and disorientated. None of the guys liked working on the place and all were very uneasy being in there by themselves.

My brother John installed an interior alarm system, and while testing the wiring with dad, there was a massive crashing noise and the sound of animal's scratching around. This made them bolt out of the house, with John vowing never to return, and he never did.

After remedial works were complete, I moved in, but it didn't take long for my "house friends" to make themselves known on a regular basis. Michelle, my girlfriend, spent a lot of time with me in the house and we both witnessed its weird activity together. One morning, at eight o'clock, we were in the bathroom on ground level when we heard loud and distinctive footsteps above our heads, crossing from one side of the room to the other.

My haunted thatched cottage, built circa 1653

We were both glued to the spot, unable to move, while our eyes slowly followed, step by step, right across the ceiling. We both distinctly heard the steps and knew we were completely alone in the house, or so we thought.

On one evening, an arrangement was made with Paul, Michelle's older brother, to pick up a set of car keys at seven the next morning. So we placed the keys on the small windowsill next to the door and retired to bed. The next morning Paul arrived on time and still half asleep, Michelle reached out for the keys but they were nowhere to be found. Paul came in to the house and Michelle shouted to wake me. It took us fifteen minutes to recover the keys. They were eventually found in the bathroom, under the towels. Now I know that most folk have these sort of things happen occasionally, and one or two we can put down to absent mindedness, but when they keep coming, and coming, then it builds, and the place starts to have depressing or depleting character, or "presence", which is a better - though often misused – word.

Tuesdays and Thursdays were very regular days for the tinkling of glasses that vibrated loudly around the house. The noise was similar to when a wine glass is struck with a fast flick of a finger and keeps reverberating for several seconds.

Not long after I had purchased the property, I placed an advert in my local paper asking for anybody with historic knowledge on the house to get in touch. I received a call from an elderly gentleman and arrangements were made for him to visit. He explained that he used to live in the house during the Second World War and when I quizzed him on ghosts at first he was reluctant to talk. He was an educated and reserved man but after a cup of hot tea and some biscuits he admitted that he had several experiences in the house, including the "tinkling of glasses". Maybe this could be a psychic replay, or an echo first sounded from the time when the cottage served as a coaching inn, when many a traveller would have been toasted *"Bon voyage!"*

In the early hours one morning, Michelle woke, as she needed to use the bathroom. She would not go downstairs alone after dark so I got up and escorted her to the bathroom, reluctantly. On the way past the lounge, I decided to check my telephone answering machine. I had to pass the coal burning fire, which radiated heat to both rooms, and as I passed the fire I walked into an icy cold spot. I said nothing as Michelle was following close behind me. As she walked into the cold spot she screamed out loud. I was not startled, but I was now **"wide-awake".** The cold spot, I'm sure, was some form of an energy presence. I put my hand in and out several times to test it. The area covered was about one metre in diameter, but I did not check its height. Michelle was really upset and I didn't want to keep her there so we went to the bathroom together, but on our return to bed, I just had to experience it one more time. Unfortunately – or fortunately – it had disappeared, and the room was back to normal, with the exception of a photograph in a frame that had been knocked off a cabinet onto the floor.

On another occasion, Michelle and I we were together in my office having a telephone conversation with Michelle's mum. Michelle was sitting by my side when we both heard a scampering of paws on the timber floor in the next room – dog paws? We were concerned as our dog, Trixie, was still only a little pup and we didn't want her to fall down the spiral staircase, so I put Michelle's mum on hold, and got up quickly to check. To our surprise, little Trixie was fast asleep under my chair! Months later I had problems with the external sewer, and when we were digging the earth to replace the drain, I discovered in the mud nearby a plastic bag containing the remains of a small buried dog. Could this have been the spirit of the dog that we had heard in the cottage?

A very scary incident occurred on three separate occasions while Michelle and I were sleeping. It was in the early hours when Michelle shook me to wake me up. She whispered, "Can you hear that?" I came to my senses rather quickly, and very clearly I could hear a woman crying, sobbing her heart out. It was happening in our bedroom and it lasted for several minutes and then faded away. As you can imagine, this really disturbed us for several days.

Michelle was again shaken one night a few weeks later when we were lying in bed, dog tired, just about to fall asleep, when Michelle screamed out hysterically and I had to shake her to get her to her senses. Michelle was facing my back and she saw a baby's arm draped over my shoulder. After a period of several minutes she was able to talk about what she had seen and described the arm as glowing like an x-ray image and it remained there until she screamed then it simply disappeared.

On another night, my good friend, Blakey, stayed over. Due to all the ongoing renovation works, he was sleeping in a sleeping bag and made himself as comfortable as possible on the floor in the lounge. After retiring, within twenty minutes Blakey shouted upstairs to me, "Alan there is someone in the house!" And he ran outside to fetch a baseball bat from his car. When he dashed back in, ready for a scrap, with a smiling face I said, "Its okay, mate, it's only the ghost." Tee-total Blakey was shaking from head to foot; he insisted he had heard someone or something walking in the room above him. I invited him to bring his sleeping bag up to my bedroom and sleep on my bedroom floor. A similar strange thing happened when another friend stayed over. He tried to light up a cigarette and the match was blown out twice. He did not attempt it a third time.

Aunty Mary and Sheila are my mother's aunties. Mary is also very sensitive or, as some say, psychic. They came to visit me in the house and Mary instantly picked up on its psychic activity. She told me that several ghosts were in the property and one was a lady named Ruth. She said that Ruth was dressed in tweed clothes and was well respected in the area; however, she had an illegitimate child. Mary received a vision of the child playing on a swing in the garden. She insisted the ghosts were happy sharing the property with me but there was also a darker side to the house. Mary picked up that black magic had been practised in the house hundreds of years ago.

One night Michelle and I were fast asleep and at about three o'clock in the morning we both woke up at the same time. I said to Michelle, "I have just had a bad dream". Michelle replied, "So have I." I asked her what she was dreaming about and she said, "I dreamt about one of your friends." I replied, "That's strange. I have just dreamt about my friend, Steven [name changed for reasons of confidentiality]." "This is really weird," said Michelle, and by now we were both sitting up in bed, wide awake.

I asked her what her dream was about and she said Steven had gone to prison. I replied, "Wow, I have just dreamt the exact dream." So, remarkably, we had both awoken at the same time, dreaming the same dream, about the same person going to prison!

At the time, it seemed impossible that it would come to any sort of fruition as Steven was a genuinely nice fellow who would avoid trouble at all cost. We didn't tell him about our dream, but I often wonder what would have happened and how he would have taken it if we had told him – it may have totally altered the course of events. However, we did tell other mutual friends. One year later, I switched on the TV to watch the local news and Steven's face was splashed all over the screen. He had been arrested for possession of millions of counterfeit U.S. dollars!

Our shared dream was a genuine precognition. It did not arise out of any suspicions that either Michelle or I consciously had of the guy, and a year later it had come true. Steven went to prison for several months. He would have received a longer sentence but the police had used entrapment in Spain to capture him. Also involved with the plot was another friend, who I shall call Peter. Peter was the printer that manufactured the counterfeit notes and he has printed all my business stationery since the first day I went into business. His work was always very good, apparently like the bank notes.

I was scared of the unexplained – or "paranormal" events – taking place in my home, and it bothered me. Although it fascinated me, too, I could never really relax there and I always felt that the house did not totally belong to me. After two years, it was time to move on and I took steps to sell the house. I buried a stainless steel time capsule deep in the sandstone structure which contained a short biography and a few small, unneeded, day-to-day items. The Old Thatched Cottage is a Grade II listed building, protected by law, and will never be demolished, so I like to think that there is now also a little part of me still in the house, and always will be.

My Much Loved Nan

It was an extremely sad time when my Nan died in March 1988. Our whole family experienced this as a tremendous loss and we each grieved in our own way. Several months after Nan passed, my cousin, David Morris, was visiting Alan, her husband, to check on his wellbeing. As Alan opened the door of the small bungalow, Dave stepped into the hall and gazed into the living room. To his amazement he saw, quite clearly sitting in her armchair, holding her walking stick – and with a nice smile on her face – our much loved Nan. Dave said that he held this vision for a good fifteen or so seconds before she disappeared.

The Man that Disappeared

My younger brother John had an unusual experience whilst out walking in Snowdonia, North Wales. Taking advantage of a superb summer's evening, he decided to walk up Snowdon, by the classic Crib Goch route. As expected and planned for, the mountain was quickly becoming free of walkers. Travelling at speed on the rugged and popular track, he met various parties, descending in the late afternoon sun. At around 5:45 p.m., roughly one kilometre from the start of the route, he saw a figure up ahead on the track. He quickly caught up with the slow moving figure and glanced upon what was before him.

The man was slightly shorter than John's own 5' 8" frame, dressed in worn-out dark clothes, the origin and fashion of which was most certainly not of this or any of the previous few decades. But it was not just the clothes, the rolled up sheet of what appeared to be plastic slung over his shoulder supported by hemp cord, or the drooped hand clasping an orange and sandwiches that made him suspect something was not quite normal – it was mostly the absence of a complexion on what was an ashen face, curtained by long, greasy, black hair.

John's initial concern was that the man might be caught out on the mountain overnight without any suitable equipment. In an attempt to find out more about this strange situation, he exchanged more than the usual brief pleasantry.

"Hello," said John.

"Rrrr," replied the man.

"You off to catch the sunset on the summit, too?"

No response. A couple of slow paces further on, wondering if the man was dressed to do work, John asked, "You off to do some path work?" John was aware that there were path repairs ahead of them.

"Nah, just up."

The conversation continued in a similar, markedly one-sided vein for a few paces more when John, still not fully aware of the situation, exchanged final pleasantries and continued on.

Some 30 metres further up the track, reflecting upon the unusual and bizarre experience, he sensed nothing about what he had just witnessed added up and turned around to look. The man was nowhere to be seen. The track at this point was on a moderate incline, unusually straight for the terrain and, most importantly, not surrounded by any cover into which the man could have disappeared. John was at a small promontory, overlooking the track from where he had just had the encounter. The only movement he could see was that of a few sheep, lower down the hillside, and despite a five minute wait, there was no sign of the *disappearing man*.

John had another similar experience while assisting dad repair a goods lift at the British Leather Company in Birkenhead, Wirral, during the summer holiday factory closure. British Leather was situated next to the world famous Cammell Laird shipyard. When looking out of the lift shaft in the general direction of the shipyard, John saw an image of a man walk the length of a newly constructed brick wall then fade and disappear.

The Haunted Staircase

My father worked as an engineer and had his own company, Wirral Lift Repairs. His primary work was to fit, remove and service stair lifts for the elderly and disabled. One day, he was fitting a lift into a large house in an affluent part of Oxton, Wirral. The job was going to plan and the lift was almost successfully installed when something very strange happened. Dad was alone in the house, and while fitting a new section of wooden stair landing, his jigsaw power tool switched itself on. Dad rushed to switch it off in a confused state. At the same time, he felt very uneasy with the atmosphere around him and just wanted to complete the job and leave. Five minutes later, the same thing happened and the jigsaw switched itself on again. Dad was getting really annoyed and shouted to the ghostly perpetrator, "Stop messing around!" The ghost must have taken heed as the power tool remained silent and the installation was completed.

Haunted Birkenhead Priory

Michelle and I experienced another ghostly encounter together at the old Birkenhead Priory, Wirral. The Priory was built in the early 12th century. Here, Benedictine monks from Chester earned a living by trading with the merchants in Liverpool and operated a ferry across the River Mersey. The priory was visited twice by Edward the 1st of England.

Michelle and I were walking around the old crypt, enjoying the history,

Paranormal activity at Birkenhead priory

when we walked into a very strange atmosphere. We both looked at each other and, from past experience, we knew it was a "cold spot". It was a very similar experience to the one we witnessed at the Old Thatched Cottage, except this was during daytime and with other tourists present.

The monks at Birkenhead Priory continued ferrying passengers to Liverpool until 1536 when the priory was closed by order of Henry VIII's bailiff, Randle Arrowesmith, and the monks returned to Chester. The priory has remained closed ever since, but Wirral's local authority has opened the crypt as a small museum and is a beautiful place to visit if you are in the area.

Michelle has had several ghostly sightings and experiences, including seeing her great grandfather smoking a cigarette. It was in the early hours of the morning when Michelle was awakened by the sound of voices. She clearly heard both a male and a female voice, the female voice prompting the male by saying, "You tell her. Go on, tell her." By now, Michelle was fully awake and sitting upright in bed and, to her amazement, six feet away was a middle aged man, dressed in a smart white suit, smoking a cigarette. The vision was as clear as day. The invisible female's voice continued to prompt the man, using the same words. The man just winked and the image slowly faded away. Michelle, for some unknown reason, did not feel frightened in any way. On the contrary, she felt pleasantly relaxed and went back to sleep. The next morning at breakfast, Michelle told her story to her mother and, after describing the appearance of the man, Michelle's mother Jean responded, with a very serious look on her face. "That was your great grandfather you saw last night!"

Michelle landed a promotional job in Manchester, working for British Rail, which meant she had to commute daily by train from Liverpool to Manchester. The passengers on the train were mainly commuting businessmen and after boarding the train at Manchester for her return leg, she started to look for an empty compartment, rather than sit with a lot of strange men. A young attractive lady made eye contact with Michelle as she passed by the first carriage, but Michelle carried on walking. After searching for several minutes for a vacant compartment, she decided to return to the first compartment where she had seen the female. As Michelle opened the door, the lady beckoned her with a smile into the compartment, but as she turned around the lady vanished into thin air. Michelle later discovered, after some research, that a young lady had been murdered on that very train.

Old Bob

My son, Jay, experienced a powerful paranormal experience at the age of nine. Jay lives with his mum, Michelle, and stepfather, "Jono", in a Victorian house in a pleasant cul-de-sac in West Kirby, Wirral. Jay had been playing in the street on a bright and sunny summer day in 2009, when he saw "Old Bob", an elderly resident who lived directly opposite Jay, walking towards his house. Bob always took an interest in Jay and they would often talk about school, striking up a conversation whenever their paths crossed. This day was no different, and as Bob passed him, he said, "Hello, Jay." Jay replied, "Hi, Bob." This was the end of the pleasantries and Bob continued his short walk to his home.

It was only when Jay was later called in for lunch that he realised that the conversation that he had earlier with Old Bob was not a normal conversation. Jay's mum asked him what he was doing in the street and Jay replied, "Just the usual things," and that he had just exchanged greetings with Old Bob. Michelle dropped the lunch plate she was holding in total shock. Jay had been totally unaware of the fact that Old Bob had died three weeks earlier!

The Ghosts on the Roof

During school term time, the week before the start of the summer holiday, in 2008, my daughter Estelle, just eight years old, was waiting in line for the annual group school photograph. The day was not unlike any other school day, except the sun was shining and the teacher was assisting the photographer to arrange the group in orderly fashion for the picture. Estelle was facing forward for the photograph when she saw an old lady standing up on the school roof and quite calmly holding and stroking Estelle's dog, "Pascha". Estelle was shocked as the dog had only recently died, and she burst out crying, running to tell her teacher. But other children, overhearing her say what she had seen, started calling her "weird" and other names, and she got so upset that the teachers sent her home for the rest of the day.

At home, while she was explaining to her mother Amanda what had happened, Amanda opened a draw in the sideboard and then gently placed an old photograph on the table in front of her. Instantly, Estelle recognised the face in the photo to be the lady on the roof. The old lady in the image and the old lady she had seen was her great grandmother, Audrey Buckley, who had passed over years before Estelle was born – and, of course, her recently deceased pet dog, Pascha, was obviously being very well looked after.

One year later, in 2009, Estelle was woken up in the early hours of the morning by a noise in her bedroom. The room was dark but the small gap in the curtains gave the room just a small amount of light to see by, and a strange presence hung over the room. Moments later, she turned over in bed, as if to go back to sleep, when she saw a little boy aged about three, walking towards her. The little boy did not scare her at all, and she remembers the lost look on his face. Just as Estelle managed to utter the words, "Who are you?" he instantly disappeared!

The Haunted Oxton Old Hall

One of the strongest ghostly encounters I ever experienced was while visiting The Oxton Old Hall, Wirral. I was viewing with an interest to buy when, casually, I asked the owner "Does the house have a ghost?" The lady was rather taken back and didn't quite know how to answer the question and the conversation was changed rather quickly. During the guided tour, I walked into the main bedroom and I was overwhelmed by a very strong presence, and it got even stronger as I walked into the en-suite bathroom. I was feeling almost dizzy, it was so powerful; the lady now realised that I was "open" to these channels and then admitted that there was a ghost of a young girl present in that room. My mother had accompanied me on the house viewing but felt nothing at all. I also experienced a strange echo whilst walking in the rear garden, almost like I was standing in a time void but I was standing in an open space.

During the first stages of legal conveyance, it was discovered that the government had marked the site as an area of archaeological importance. I did not buy the house in the end and, with hindsight, I am glad that I didn't. It does not end here, as coincidence has it that the man who eventually purchased the Old Hall was the director of the company that published my first book, *Hypnotic Star*! He was surprised to read this story of his home during the printing process.

The Ghost of Helena

While renovating my home, The Old School House, I was cleaning up the plasterwork and rubbish off the lounge floor when the hair on the back of my neck started to rise. I could sense the presence of an old lady. It was a kind feeling that I received and so I spoke out to her, saying how I was looking forward to living in the house and that she was very welcome to share the home with me. Over several years of living in the Old School House, a few people, without any prompting, have picked up the presence of an old lady in the corner in the same room in a rocking chair. And when spirit medium, Derek Acorah, and his wife, Gwen, stayed over one night, Derek actually made contact with her, and she told him she used to live in the house and her name was Helena.

Friendly Warning

Days before the break up with my partner, Alnifa, I was spooked by several ghostly goings on at my home. Emotional times and periods of intense feelings seem to trigger links and spiritual contact; perhaps they make us more aware or open to subtle effects. My bedside table light had switched itself on. At first I dismissed it, thinking that I had put it on without consciously realising it, but when it happened a second time I started paying attention. I went to work the following evening and deliberately switched the lamp off from the wall socket as well as the lamp switch. On my arrival home that night after work, I had forgotten all about the lamp and made my way to my bedroom. I opened the door and to my shock and amazement the light had been switched on, both at the power point and the switch! I look back now and thank the powers that be for the "friendly warning". Very similar things have happened to me over the years since and not unlike the wailing warnings of "banshees" from old legends, they are warning me for a reason.

The Ability to Sense a Presence

I have also used this ability of being able to sense a presence in a property. Ralf and Wendy Sergeant had poltergeist activity in their home in Bebington, Wirral, and invited me over to "have a feel". I walked around the house with them and we all remained silent until the end of the tour. I had picked up on an unusual feeling in the kitchen area, and when the tour had finished and they asked what I thought, I told them of my feelings about the kitchen, and they confessed that I was correct and that articles were being thrown around that room.

I also had a similar experience when I was interested in purchasing yet another "old" property, the Old Rectory, from the Chester diocese. It is just that I find old houses have more charm and character, and usually also feel more welcoming to me; that is, I suppose they "feel" good – warm and homely – "good vibes", as people say, and surely here we are talking about the same sensitivity and "open" quality that this whole chapter is outlining.

The rectory was the home of my now late friend, Reverend Andrew Dean. It dated back to the reign of Queen Anne and was considered too big and costly for the diocese to maintain. I viewed the property and generally felt the house had a wealth of warmth and character. However, one bedroom in particular had a very strange feeling to it. So, before I went any further with the purchase, I arranged for my friend, the spirit medium Derek Acorah, to take a look around – a sort of "spectral survey" you might say. We toured the house together, during which I remained silent. At the end of the tour, Derek had picked up that there was a presence in the house in the form of an old departed vicar, and he was in the very same bedroom that I had identified. As it turned out, the diocese kept hold of the property and I missed out on this beautiful ancient dwelling.

The Ghost Boy of Caer Rhun Hall

I was booked on Friday, 27th September, 2002, to do a private show for twenty doctors at Caer Rhun Hall, Conwy, in North Wales. Caer Rhun Hall is built on the former Roman fortress site known as Canovium and is situated five miles outside Conwy in very beautiful grounds. The hall is very old and was originally built for a General Gough – one can imagine the stories it could tell.

Due to traffic problems, I arrived later than I had anticipated but was warmly welcomed by the dinner party host and directed to the room in which I was to perform, after the docs had finished dining. I then asked the host for a dressing room and she escorted me to the library. As I stepped into the room, I instantly picked up on a very strong presence, the hair

Haunted, Caer Rhun Hall Conwy

on the back of my neck was standing on end. I felt disoriented to a point that I had to leave the room quickly, after hanging up my stage suit.

After completing my performance and demonstration, I was sitting with the chef in the kitchen and I asked him if the hall was haunted (knowing only too well there was something going on). The chef nodded and replied, "Yes, it's the ghost of a little boy who has been seen by many different guests. The story goes that the little ghost boy had played cards with the young son of one of the former guests." I then asked the question I'd been leading up to. "So which is the haunted room then?" To this, he replied with a grin, "The library that you are using for a dressing room."

Trixie Returns

Three months after the death of my dog and best friend, Trixie, I was awakened by something trying to get into my bed. I had found Trixie in a dog rescue home, and during thirteen years of companionship, she virtually never left my side. Trixie was extremely intelligent and appeared at times to think on a human level. Michelle, my wife at the time, was away working in Florida and I was alone in bed – or so I thought. As I lifted the duvet cover, cuddled up to me, and staring at me with beautiful loving eyes, was my dear Trixie. I was not frightened at all. On the contrary, I was now sitting upright in bed, more than wide-

Best friend Trixie, Liverpool Echo, 2002

awake, and to prove I was not dreaming, I pinched myself very hard several times. I held the vision without blinking for what seemed like ages but in reality was around thirty seconds. Eventually, the vision faded and the duvet was left shaped in the form of Trixie. It was a very pleasant experience!

Hypnotic Séance

During the time I lived at the Old School House, Arrowe Park, Wirral, I was invited to participate in a TV documentary with a popular medium, Gary Dakin, from Manchester. My part in the programme was to hypnotise Gary and assist him to travel deeper in trance, using my skills as a hypnotist. The séance started with heavy breathing before Gary's eyes rolled back in their sockets. His complexion became ashen white and he started talking in a totally different voice, which seemed completely out of synchronisation with his facial movements. Saliva continually ran down from both sides of his mouth as he sat very still, mouth wide open. As this was my first time witnessing such a physical response in a medium, the whole event was very scary.

The voice that came through was certainly not anything like the voice of Gary Dakin. It told me that I was having serious problems with my stomach. There was nothing I knew of this at the time, but in the future I would need lifesaving stomach surgery.

The spirit voice finished by saying, "The Earth is going to be hit by an asteroid in the future." It followed this up with, "You are not ready for this." Gary then started to awake from the trance state and his complexion returned to normal. He wiped his mouth and took a few minutes to regain his senses. Afterwards, he said that he remembered nothing at all of the event and that he never did.

Bet on a Spooky Winner

One day while living in the Old Thatched Cottage, a strange old man approached as Michelle and I walked out of the front gate. The man pointed to a shirt I was wearing and informed me that "Chaplin's" was going to win today and walked off. "What a peculiar chap!" I remarked to Michelle. I was wearing a T-shirt given to me by the owner of the restaurant named Chaplin's in Birkenhead. I wondered what on earth the old man was talking about. Michelle said jokingly, "Maybe it's a horse that will win today." We knew nothing about horse racing and we had never been inside a betting shop, but we decided we had to investigate further.

So off we went into the local betting shop and enquired if a horse called Chaplin's was running that day? After checking, the lady assistant replied, "Yes, this afternoon." Michelle and I thought it was such a strange coincidence that we had to place a two-pound bet on the horse. The next day, we went back to the betting shop with our receipt and, to our amazement, the horse had won the race with fabulous odds!

In the next chapter, I give a diary memo style account of strange incidents that happened from the year 2008 up to the writing of this book. You now have the overwhelming desire to turn the page …

CHAPTER EIGHT
GHOST DIARY

In December 2008, due to the amount of strange and unusual things that were happening in my life, I decided to make a memo style diary entry for any unexplainable phenomena. Before any entry was made, every incident was investigated fully for rational explanation. I would like to make an observation at this point that strange activity tends to happen more frequently when I am with another person, particularly my ex-wives. I am pleased this is so as having a witness to the events proves that I am not imagining it. My ex-wives are both sensitive and maybe the joining of our energies is the reason why so many anomalies were witnessed together.

I wish I had started this memo diary at an earlier date as now lots of esoteric and strange experiences are lost from memory. What I began to accept as normal maybe you, the reader, may treat as not so normal, or even paranormal. Please, be my judge. Thus, the following entries that have been logged have all passed my diligent tests and are worthy for your perusal. I hope you find them interesting.

December 26th, 2008. Time: 22.15 hrs. Location: Port Sunlight home.

In bed watching a movie on TV when my wife Steph's mobile phone rang. I muted the TV and the display showed the number dialling as our home number. Upon answering the phone the line was dead. We were the only souls in the house, or so we thought.

December 29th, 2008. Time: unknown. Location: Port Sunlight home.

Paranormal activity at Port Sunlight home

I smelled very strong cigarette smoke in Keira's bedroom (100% house policy: no smokers allowed into our home).

December 30th, 2008. Time: 22.15 hrs. Location: Port Sunlight home.

Keira woke up screaming, "Mummy!" Steph rushed into her bedroom and found Keira cowering in the bottom of her cot, shaking and crying, "Mummy, Mummy!" The dream-catcher decoration which was attached to the curtain pole was swinging from side to side (there are no draughts in room) and again a strong smell of cigarettes. Keira would not calm down and had to be taken out of the room. (Note the time: 22.15).

January 1st, 2009. Time: 20.04 hrs. Location: Port Sunlight home.

Another very strong smell of cigarette smoke in the living room, this time witnessed by Steph, Steph's mum, "Sylv", and myself.

January 17th, 2009. Time: 21.00 hrs. Location: Port Sunlight home.

Located at the bottom of a very steep set of stairs leading from the first floor to the attic rooms was a child safety gate to protect our young daughter Keira ascending and, more importantly, falling down the stairs. The gate was new but required a spot of oil as whenever it was opened it made a distinctive loud squeak. We were very cautious regarding this gate and it was **never** left open.

The staircase was positioned outside the bathroom door and while Keira was fast asleep in bed I was soaking in a hot bath. Steph and I were holding a conversation when we both heard the distinctive sound of the stair safety gate squeak open. Steph jumped up and ran out of the bathroom and to her amazement the gate was wide open.

March 18th, 2009. Time: 20.09 hrs. Location: Port Sunlight home.

While watching Keira play with her toys Sylv, Keira and I witnessed a very strong smell of cigarettes and this smell lingered for five minutes.

April 14th, 2009. Time: 19.00 hrs. Location: Port Sunlight home.

While watching TV in the conservatory, the TV switched channels on its own. When Steph switched it off as she left the room, the TV came back on again.

April 18th, 2009. Time: 21.30 hrs. Location: Jay's home, West Kirby.

Jay, my son was with his mother at their home when a plastic water bottle flew across the kitchen from one end to the other and hit Jay on his shoulder. The bottle changed its course in mid-flight.

June 2nd, 2009. Time: 13.17 hrs. Location: Port Sunlight home.

I was at my desk, working in my office, when I distinctly heard two people whispering very close to me. I was the only person in the house.

July 28th, 2009. Time: 20.30 hrs. Location: Port Sunlight home.

At home, sitting on the bed with Steph and Keira. Keira was staring and pointing in the corner of the room saying, "Lady".

August 14th, 2009. Time: 20.55 hrs. Location: Port Sunlight home.

Relaxing in the living room with Jay when he saw a purple light flash across the room.

August 26th, 2009. Time: 23.25 hrs. Location: Port Sunlight home.

Steph heard whispering on the first floor landing twice, emanating from the bathroom.

December 13th, 2009. Time: 22.30 hrs. Location: Port Sunlight home.

Steph and I smelled cigarette smoke in the same part of the living room, and as on past occasions, it dissipated after several minutes.

January 12th, 2010. Time: 16.00 hrs. Location: Greendale Road junction with Ellen's Lane, Port Sunlight Village, Wirral.

This diary entry is rated my *"number one paranormal experience"*. It was a shared experience and should have been written into the previous chapter, "The Spirit World".

Location of ghost lady drive through, January 2010

Steph and I were driving on Greendale Road in our picturesque village of Port Sunlight, Wirral. The weather conditions on the day were cold and dry with good visibility. Just as we turned right under the brick constructed railway bridge arch, (as seen in picture) an old lady dressed in out-of-date clothes, an old brown coat and white headscarf was standing in a stooped position in the middle of the road, head bent over. She was on the wrong side of the road, which had no pavement. The narrow carriageway had two lanes only so I had to swerve to miss her, but failed. I was restricted on the road due to the bridge wall on my left side and the line of stationary traffic queuing at the junction on my right and so drove straight through her.

This should have resulted in the woman's certain death. I stopped the car ten meters past the bridge. However, looking back over my shoulder, the old lady was still there, standing in the middle of the road, and in the same position! Steph and I both looked at each other in utter shock and disbelief; we had both witnessed this unbelievable apparition!

February 18th, 2010. Time: 17.20 hrs. Location: Port Sunlight home.

I arrived home with Keira after shopping and carried her into the house. Steph gave her a hug and her hair smelled of cigarette smoke. We had no contact with any smokers nor been anywhere near a smoker's location.

February 19th, 2010. Time: 04.20 hrs. Location: Port Sunlight home.

Keira woke up crying and I went to console her. The room smelled of cigarette smoke, especially around the top part of her bed and on Keira.

February 20th, 2010. Time: 19-30 hrs. Location: Port Sunlight home.

Steph and I returned home from a restaurant and our bedroom smelled very strongly of cigarettes. The smell lingered for approximately 15 minutes.

March 17th, 2010. Time: 11.30 hrs. Location: Port Sunlight home.

I was in my office and I thought about an idiot of a man that had visited my home several months ago via the estate agents with a view to buy. I dismissed him as a time-waster and a fool. As I was thinking about him, my phone rang and it was the estate agent, Cathy Behan, asking for an appointment for the same goon who wanted a second viewing.

April 6th, 2010. Time: 18.30 hrs. Location: Port Sunlight home.

Steph smelled strong cigarette smoke in the kitchen.

April 7th, 2010. Time: 14.00 hrs. Location: Port Sunlight home.

The living room chandelier light switched itself on.

July 30th, 2010. Time: 19.45 hrs. Location: Port Sunlight home.

Steph had put Keira to bed and, while lying with her, Steph, with her eyes closed, sensed a bright light in front of her face. At the same time, something blew on her forehead. She opened her eyes and everything was normal.

August 1st, 2010. Time: 14.35 hrs. Location: Merseyside train network, Liverpool to West Kirby, Wirral line.

My son Jay was travelling home with his mum and grandmother on the train from Liverpool, after shopping, and sitting opposite them was a Chinese lady, aged in her sixties. Jay was sitting next to his grandmother while Michelle, his mum, was sitting in a different part of the train. After making eye contact with Jay and his grandmother, the lady simply vanished from her seat in front of them.

August 28th, 2010. Time 14.15 hrs. Location: Northop, North Wales.

While attending a BBQ at the house of my brother John and wife Kate, Keira asked about a little baby boy who was sitting on the grass next to Amber. There was no baby boy. Keira also talked about a man with green eyes that visits her at night.

December 20th, 2010. Time: 17.00 hrs. Location: Port Sunlight home.

Steph was tidying Keira's bedroom while Keira was

entertaining herself bouncing on the bed when suddenly the bedroom light switched itself off. The switch construction is a dimmer switch that needs to be physically pushed on / off.

Later that evening at 21.15 hrs, Steph stepped out of the shower when she heard an adult voice whisper, "Dad, Dad" from outside the bathroom door! Both our daughters, Keira and Amber, were in bed fast asleep.

January 13th, 2011. Time: 22.30 hrs. Location: Port Sunlight home.

On the carpet in the hallway, in-between the bedrooms on the first floor, a handful of biscuit crumbs strangely materialised in a neat pile. Both children were in bed fast asleep. I had passed between rooms several times, checking on the children after they had gone to sleep, and I knew for sure that the biscuits were not on the floor at any time.

February 22th, 2011. Time: circa 08.00hrs. Location: Port Sunlight home.

Steph and baby Amber were in bed watching Pepper Pig on DVD when the volume on the DVD player increased from 8 to 12 on the volume scale. Steph had to get out of bed to turn it down manually.

Later in the day, at 18.17 hrs, a large antique picture of ancient Liverpool, which hung securely above the kitchen sink, came crashing down on to the floor. The robust fittings were all completely intact.

May 25th, 2011. Time: 06.20hrs. Location: Port Sunlight home.

Steph woke up at her usual time (above) and went downstairs to the kitchen. Out of nowhere a voice called out just once to her:

153

"Steph". She thought it was me and came back upstairs to find both children fast asleep and our bedroom door firmly closed.

October 6th, 2012. Time: 10.30 hrs. Location: Carnsdale Road, Moreton.

A clock above the fireplace mysteriously moved forward by one hour without human interference. It was not due to the shift from GMT and the clock is a sturdy reliable timepiece.

March 27th, 2013. Time: 20.25 hrs. Location: The Imperial Hotel Sliema, Malta.

While visiting the Imperial Hotel in Rudolph Street, Triq Il, Kullegg, in a corridor a few yards away from the main reception area, I sensed a very strong presence which made me feel dizzy. I spoke with the concierge and explained my feelings. He confirmed a variety of ghosts, including a man and a little boy, had been seen several times in the same area. During the night shift when everyone is sleeping, the duty managers have experienced many strange noises and shadows that cannot be explained. I have since returned to the hotel on several occasions but the corridor was devoid of any presence.

May 19th, 2014. Time: between 04.00 hrs – 06.00 hrs. Location: room 430 Victoria Hotel, Sliema, Malta.

I was in Malta on my regular monthly working visits and, during the early hours of the morning, I was woken up by a noise coming from my dressing table area directly opposite my bed. The noise sounded like I had an intruder in my room moving items around on the table. I looked up in a sleepy state and I managed to see without switching on my bedside light that nobody else was present in the room. I went straight back to sleep. My alarm woke me for work at 08.00 a.m. Once showered and dressed, I went to put on my Cartier Panthere watch and the time read

10.32 a.m. On further investigation I found the crown winder that is used to adjust the date and time had been pulled out two stages, which is impossible to do without using your nails and physically applying some pressure. The crown winder remained out, resulting in the pausing of time, but it still does not explain the watch time of 10.32 a.m. as I was already in bed before this time? Was this the noise that woke me up and maybe perhaps a poltergeist was having fun with me?

November 13th, 2014. Time: 08.30 hrs. Location: Victoria Hotel lobby, Sliema, Malta.

After my usual breakfast routine at the Palace hotel, I made my way towards the fire exit stairs on the ground floor to walk to my office on the 1st floor. Just as I approached the solidly constructed fire door, secured by a heavy recoil spring, the door opened wide and closed on its own. As it closed, I saw the back of a lady materialise then disappear. I quickly opened the door but nobody was present. It requires a heavy hand to open the door and a draft of wind was ruled out due to fire regulations. I discussed this strange incident with the drivers of the chauffeur company that have an office opposite the fire door and one of the drivers admitted that on night duty, while the lobby was quiet, he too had seen the door open and close without human intervention.

In the next chapter I cover some very strange experiences that I witnessed with UFO's, (unexplained flying objects) and a film documentary that involved me allegedly making contact, under deep hypnosis with an alien entity, through a human host.

CHAPTER NINE
UFOs

Apart from my paranormal experiences with the spirit world, I have also witnessed several UFO incidents. But, in my opinion, I do not believe they are connected or linked with the spirit world. The term UFO is not necessarily an alien entity or spacecraft. The term is used to broadly describe any flying object that is unidentified at the time, whether it be terrestrial or extra-terrestrial; that is, earthly or from beyond, or other than earthly.

I have categorised these following events according to Dr J. Hynek's scale of UFO experiences.

Close Encounter of the Second Kind

My first encounter was on the Wirral coastline, near the old Leasowe lighthouse that I have covered in a previous chapter. I was on a date with a young lady, in the early hours, when the van we were in lit up brightly. I said to my companion, "Don't worry, it will just be the police checking up on stolen vehicles, and as we are not in a stolen vehicle we have nothing to worry about." After several minutes, the bright light which was far more than any torch or even headlights could project, continued to light up my vehicle, so I looked out the front and rear windows and, to my surprise, no other vehicles were present. We then noticed a strange ball of orange light, silently hovering above, scanning my vehicle and flooding light on the surrounding area. I said to my companion, "Perhaps it's time to go." She was in complete agreement and very quickly we left for home. After dropping my date safely back home, I myself drove home and woke my brother Gary to tell him all about my experience. But he just turned over in bed and said, "Alan, go back to sleep."

My second encounter was again around the same time period as my first experience. I was walking home at 2.30 a.m. after a night out partying in the Golden Guinea nightclub, New Brighton. I admit that I had been

Moreton beach, site of a UFO close encounter

drinking but I'm certain that alcohol played no part in what I was to see. The weather conditions were fine and very clear, there was not a cloud in the sky – the visibility was perfect. As I walked home along the seafront promenade, I noticed two lights that looked like stars, travelling at fantastic speeds from different parts of the night sky. They slowed down in what seemed an intelligent manner and conjoined with a stationary star / light in the sky. By now I was sitting down watching them. They were stationary for about a minute then the three joined lights accelerated as one and, just like a shooting star, sped off as fast as anything I have ever seen, right across the clear night sky and out of view.

My third UFO encounter took place in 1997. I was travelling home northbound on the M53 motorway after a night out at the movies with Alnifa my girlfriend. We had joined the motorway at Junction 4, Clatterbridge, Wirral, and after travelling 150 yards, a ball of strange light shot out horizontally at my car windscreen, level from the left hand side, and either imploded or exploded –

we could not be certain – and disappeared in front of our eyes. The ball of light was approximately eighteen inches in diameter. It filled perfectly the image of a plasma energy ball. These are thought to strike at the nearest conductible matter. It made no sound and it seemed to be intelligently controlled as all of its actions happened so very fast. We both looked at each other and at the same time also both exclaimed, "What!"

We decided to go back to the location and check it out. I continued to the next junction and re-entered the motorway again at Junction 4. Alnifa was anxious and worried and wanted to go home but I managed to convince her it would be safe. We drove slowly to where the incident happened and I stopped the car on the motorway's hard shoulder. I got out of my car and scrambled up the steep grass verge, but when I peered over the top, there was nothing but field after field of empty darkness, and complete silence prevailed.

The Moon's Gravitational Effects

I have my own theory on Earth's nearest neighbour, the Moon, and I have conducted limited research. The Moon controls the gravitational pull on our planet thus controlling the earth's tidal system which ebbs and flows twice in every twenty-four hour period. As the moon has this powerful control over our vast oceans, I believe it has some control and effect over our own human bodies which are also composed mainly of water. I have experienced this on so many occasions. I first noticed altered behavioural patterns with colleagues whilst working on the cruise ships. A couple of days leading up to the full moon, several of the casino staff's personalities and attitudes would change. Quite out of character, they would play jokes on each other and would became very mischievous. Mood swings were also evident.

Similarly, years later, while working as a DJ in the nightclubs, I could sense the attitude of the punters during the lead up to, and when the moon was at, its full cycle, and, well in advance, could very often predict when trouble was about to happen.

I was also friendly with a nurse who worked on a psychiatric hospital ward in North Wales, and even when the patients were safely in rooms - some even without windows – they were affected by the lead up to the full Moon. This nurse took time off sick on several occasions during this period because the patients were always very difficult to deal with. I can always tell when the moon is approaching full, even when the night sky is overcast with cloud. After checking my diary's Moon chart, I am always correct.

The Rendlesham Forest Incident

Now, it was understandable with those experiences behind me that when the opportunity came to get more involved in investigating UFOs, that I was not just interested, but that I would jump at the chance. The event that drew me and most aroused my interest, and the interest of a good number of discerning people worldwide, was the Rendlesham Forest incident.

The incident occurred in 1980, in late December, and the location was Rendlesham Forest, in Suffolk, England. Nearby RAF Woodbridge was a base utilised by the American Air Force, and it was here that what many people consider

to be the UK's most fascinating UFO incident took place. Events that happened here were on the scale of America's famous "Roswell" which, even today, after 68 years, still draws plenty of attention. I do not endeavour to cover this story in complete detail but cover only the salient points relevant to my experience. For the interested reader, it's worth spending time researching this incident as it is a fascinating story in itself, and 35 years later, not unlike Roswell, it is still a magnet for those with a passion for this particular kind of unexplained phenomena.

At 3 a.m. on 26th December, 1980, strange lights were reported by a security patrol near the East Gate of RAF Woodbridge, apparently descending into nearby Rendlesham Forest. Servicemen initially thought it was a downed aircraft, but upon entering the forest to investigate they saw – according to the Deputy Base Lt. Col. Charles Halt's memo: a strange glowing object, metallic in appearance, with coloured lights. As they approached, it moved through the trees, and "the animals on a nearby farm went into a frenzy". The craft left three impressions, or depressions, in the ground, which were visible the next day. One of the servicemen, Sergeant Jim Penniston, allegedly claimed to have encountered a "craft of unknown origin" and to have made detailed notes of its features, touched its "warm" surface, and copied the numerous symbols on its body. The object reportedly flew away after their brief encounter. Shortly after 4 a.m., local British police were called to the scene but reported that the only lights they could see were those from the lighthouse some miles away on the coast.

After daybreak on the morning of 26th December, servicemen returned to a small clearing near the eastern edge of the forest and found three small impressions in a triangular pattern, as well as burn marks and broken branches on nearby trees. At 10.30 a.m., the local police were called out again, this time to see the impressions on the ground. Several servicemen and Lt. Col. Charles Halt returned to the site again in the early hours of 28th December with radiation detectors. Halt investigated this sighting personally and recorded the events on a micro-cassette recorder. It was during this investigation that a flashing light was seen across the field to the east, almost in line with a farmhouse. The Orford Ness lighthouse is visible further to the east in the same line of sight. Later, star like lights were seen in the sky to the north and south, the brightest of which seemed to beam down a stream of light from time to time. There are claims that the incident was videoed by the U.S. Air Force; but, if so, the resulting tape has not been made public.

Thirty years later I was approached by Paul Wookey, a TV presenter and film-maker with a keen interest in the paranormal. Paul had gathered a team that included Lt. Col. Charles Halt (USAF, retired deputy base commander), Nick Pope,[1] formerly the UK Ministry of Defence's own UFO "X-files" style investigator (1985 to 2006), TV presenter Emily Booth, the psychic medium, Christine Hamlett Walsh, and myself. The objective was to produce a TV documentary and to try and uncover what really happened on those dark nights in December 1980. By utilising all of our talents we hoped to probe deeper and, once and for all, resolve the file on Rendlesham on its 30th anniversary.

Apart from the United States military witnesses, there are other local English witnesses who claim not only to have seen what is already out in the public domain, but also to have actually been abducted and still to be in contact with their abductors. My input in this exciting documentary was to hypnotise and regress a local lady named Brenda.

Brenda seriously believes that aliens regularly make contact with her. She was willing for me to hypnotise her and regress her to this time period, and also – if permission was granted under hypnosis – to communicate with her alien associates. This was the first time I was to do something like this. I was very excited with the prospect of involving hypnosis in the investigation, and also of speaking with an "alien" by using a human as a host. To me, something had happened that night that must have been extraordinary – beyond the ordinary – and I was very interested in finding out what it could be.

We conducted the session at Brenda's home. Once the production team and cameramen were set to go, I successfully hypnotised the subject and guided her into a very deep trance state. Brenda relived her first close encounter and abduction in the forest and this was really fascinating to listen to. This was similar in many ways to past life regression – notes were being taken, and video and audio records were being made to catch any verifiable evidence that the witness can relate to be collaborated later. But what happened next gave me a jolt. Under deep hypnosis I asked if it were possible for me to communicate with her alien associate. Brenda's voice paused for a minute and then she spoke. Permission was granted and, from that point, I was "allegedly" communicating with an entity from another world. Just as when I had hypnotised medium Gary Dakin during the trance séance, the synchronising of the actual voice box with the muscles in the mouth and throat where not in tune or alignment. It is possible for humans to do this voluntarily but very difficult; you would really have to practice. To give you an example of what I witnessed, it was like watching a good ventriloquist doing very unnatural things yet producing a natural though disassociated flow of words, if you can understand. Here, the voice was completely different to Brenda's and had a character and an atmosphere all its own.

The dialogue itself was interesting too. The alien informed us that they had been on Earth for centuries and that there were two types of species, which were basically at war with each other. The entity assured me that they were the peaceful ones and that the host, Brenda, was safe to be used in such a manner, though for a limited time only. My final question to the alien was, "Were you responsible for the activity in Rendlesham Forest, in December 1980?" The reply was distinctly affirmative! The several other elements of the programme contained fascinating first-hand accounts with Lt. Col. Charles Halt. This man held the highest security clearance at the time with the United States air force, and Nick Pope likewise held UK security MOD clearance.

At exactly the same time and date thirty years later, our team gathered in Rendlesham Forrest at the same location to recall step by step from Lt. Col. Halt on what really happened. There are several conspiracy theories,

Nick Pope Brenda, author & Col. Charles Halt

including the accusation of a cover-up by the US and UK military. And then here we have Lt. Col. Halt, in my opinion a man of very sound mind, intelligent and articulate, recounting exactly what happened thirty years ago on this very night.

One of the theories put forward is that the USAF were using the airbase as a storage facility for nuclear weapons, contrary to a clear denial from both the UK and US governments. I put this question to Lt. Col. Halt off camera but he refused to answer. My personal feelings are that, yes, this was a storage base for WMD, or "Weapons of Mass Destruction", which, at the time of the intense confrontations at Greenham Common, would have certainly, explained the secrecy. The nuclear weapons scenario has also been suggested as the reason for possible alien interest in the area.

Another theory is that the light they saw was the light emanating from the Orford Ness lighthouse. During our filming, the cloud visibility and weather was fair and we could clearly see the beam of light from the lighthouse. I can categorically state that in those conditions, they were nothing like the lights witnessed in 1980. The Orford light was a tiny blip in the distance and, to me, it is complete nonsense to put this theory forward.

The Rendlesham Forest incident sadly still remains a mystery and may never be solved. But, for me, I deeply enjoyed meeting and working with Lt. Col. Halt, Nick Pope and my other colleagues, and spending time on the film shoot, including my experiences with the alleged abductee, Brenda. These incidents and experiences themselves "open" our minds to new viewpoints and to question the nature of what we accept as "normal". It is my personal view that a cover-up had taken place at Rendlesham Forest and that we, mere mortals, are being shielded. But, if so, why, and for what purpose? The following information made news headlines at the time of publishing this book.

US airman John Burroughs secured the settlement after years of trying to prove his ill-health was caused by the encounter in Rendlesham Forest. A former Ministry of Defence (MoD) official said the pay-out confirms what he saw was real and had caused him physical harm.

Mr Burroughs put forward a declassified report as evidence he had been injured during the event on Boxing Day 1980. He said disability coverage from the US Veteran's Association offered "some closure", but that he now wanted unrestricted access to his full medical records.

"Every step along the way people have said it's not true. Some people will always say that.

"I don't know if I have the full answer, but no one thought I'd get this far," said the ex-servicemen. Along with Jim Penniston, he was the first to investigate mysterious lights near the East Gate of RAF Woodbridge.

Theories included the glow of Orfordness Lighthouse, an elaborate hoax and a secret classified aircraft. Lawyer Pat Frascogna, who represented the retired technical sergeant, said: "This excludes the bogus explanations put out there over the years. I cannot underscore what a major development this is. We're more curious now than ever.

"We were denied access to records, mainly dating back to 1979, which we believe would have shown John had no health problems when he entered the air force, but that he developed heart problems and other ailments that arose from the incident."

In fighting his case, Mr Burroughs used a declassified study code-named Project Condign, in which Rendlesham is described as an event where it "might be postulated that several observers were probably exposed to Unidentified Aerial Phenomena (UAP) radiation."

Mr Frascogna said: "Condign specifically mentions the incident and how radiation from unidentified aerial phenomena could cause injury.

"John was able to furnish that document, and another dating back to the incident, when a radiation reading found levels to be significantly higher than normal."

Mr Burroughs, who suffers heart problems and has a pacemaker, said: "I'm very happy we finally have some closure.

"Condign explained that there is a phenomenon that governments of this world are well aware of. The question is where it comes from."

Four years ago, the MoD released 35 archives of UFO-related documents but then revealed that papers on Rendlesham had gone missing. Mr Burroughs believes the missing files may reveal further clues.

Nick Pope, author of Encounter in Rendlesham Forest: The inside Story of the World's Best-Documented UFO Incident, worked on the government's UFO desk in the early 1990s. He said: "After years of denial this is official confirmation that what they encountered was real, and caused them physical harm.

"This welcome development doesn't give us a definitive explanation of the Rendlesham Forest incident, but it takes us ever closer to the truth."

[1] Nick Pope, Encounter in Rendlesham Forest.

CHAPTER TEN
MALTA

I would never have thought on the 19th January, 2002, after a corporate show for Malta Telecommunications, on the small island of Gozo, that Malta was to become a very important part of my life and practically, my second home. I was picked up at the airport in Malta by Marcette Busuttil. Marcette, of EM Promotions, had contracted me via my agent at the time, Entertainment UK, in London. From the airport, she drove me to the five star Corinthia hotel complex at St George's Bay, which would be my home base during the visit.

The next day we took the ferry across to the cosy island of Gozo and then on to the Kempinski San Lawrenz resort where the private function was to take place. After the sound checks were completed, and the usual pre-show run through, we checked in to the Grand Hotel and had dinner. We were then informed that I would start my show at 1.00 a.m. I was billed as a top "international surprise artist". As you can imagine, I was a little concerned as to the lateness of the show and also to the fact that all the guests were top middle-aged executives. I started "treading the boards", like so many entertainers do as ritual preparation for their stage call, including also some prayers to the "hypnotic god" that the show would be well received. (Hypnos is the name of the Greek god of sleep.)

My call time eventually arrived and I made my entrance. The guests did not have a clue what was happening, and when I asked for willing volunteers, out of 180 very elegantly dressed, mature guests, who had been seated for over six hours, nobody put their

166

hand up. Poor Marcette! Never having witnessed me performing before, and seeing that reaction, she was rather anxious to say the least. I persevered, applied my hypnotic induction, and my faithful prayers were answered: I had my required six hypnotised volunteers. From then on, the people who were about to leave for bed at this late hour were glued to their seats for my whole show. The show went very well and after the

Author & Peppi Azzopardi on set

performance we went to the Ku nightclub for well-deserved after show drinks and a de-brief on the night's performance. It was agreed that I had a hard audience but the feedback received was excellent, and so the Maltese die was now cast.

Marcette's first idea with my regard was actually not the corporate show, but to hold two shows for charity – specifically, *Razzett tal - Hbiberija* (translation: "Park of Friendship"), which was a charity offering various rehabilitation services to people with special needs. As she worked on this, she developed an idea to put me on TV through *Xarabank*, one of the most popular weekly TV shows. Marcette negotiated with Peppi Azzopardi, the presenter, to broadcast a programme featuring me in both the formats I work in, comedy hypnosis and hypnotherapy (e.g. dealing with various phobias live). However, she asked that the programme be in the form of a telethon to raise money for this charity.

The next couple of days were spent being terribly spoilt by my fabulous hosts, including a personal "after hours" guided tour around Malta's air museum, arranged by Marcette's brother,

Tonio, and the museum's dedicated volunteers. Being something of a World War II buff, I felt very privileged to be allowed to sit in the cockpit of a Spitfire – yes, a Spitfire – and was so proud to

Captain Bates at the controls of a Spitfire

hold the controls. I could only dream about what it must have been like in a dogfight with German and Italian fighters over Valletta and, indeed, England, during the Battle of Britain. I closed my eyes and, as a pilot, I drifted away to times gone by. It was a very memorable experience for me. I love that legendary plane and all it stands for. The experience brought it all back – memories of when I was pilot in command, landing an aircraft in the circuit with a Spitfire at RAF Duxford.

As a thank you to the museum, I donated to them several of my precision tools from my early apprenticeship days at DT&G, including a box of original airframe Lancaster Bomber rivets. After a truly great experience, I departed for England very much looking forward to my next return to the beautiful Malta and its marvellous people.

The time passed very quickly and on Thursday 28th February, 2002, I was back in Malta, driven straight from the airport to a boardroom meeting at the San Gorg Hotel, along with all the TV crew, including: "PJ", the director, Keith, the sound and light engineer, and presenter, Peppi Azzopardi. It now dawned on me that I was the first hypnotist for many years to come to this beautiful island and I had to fully explain in great detail, step by step, the way I thought the show should run. It was also important that although the majority of people speak fluent English, Peppi still had to translate the highlights in Maltese. After we sorted out potential problems, I retired to bed to get some necessary "shuteye" for what was to be a very busy day ahead.

Live on TV set of Xarabank

Dawn broke and after an early breakfast Marcette arrived to take me to our first engagement of the day, a live interview with Australian presenter, "Oz", on Island Sound Radio. Our next appointment was at the P.B.S. television studios to cover what we had discussed the previous night and to meet Mario, the sound engineer. Once we were all confident that we were "all on the same page" so to speak, we broke off for lunch at a nice restaurant in Medina, "the silent city". Due to Marcette's skills and hard work, the excitement that was generated in advance of my first live show on Maltese TV, and the Corinthia hotel theatre show, was now looking very positive. The atmospherics in Malta were now picking up momentum.

We arrived on time and were welcomed into a hive of activity – assistant producers, runners, security, all rushing around. The show was to be broadcast live at 8.45 p.m., the studio audience arriving at seven. Producer, John Paul Mifsud, rushed me to makeup, and then after Mario fitted my lapel microphone, I was wafted into the studio for the final sound and light check. I was very nervous, especially as this show was presented live and would be completely out of my hands. Plus, I didn't understand the Maltese language. I stepped back from it all, almost like an out-of-body-experience, and again thought to myself, "Alan, you have really come a long way since Mr. Gordon, my headmaster at school said, 'Bates, you are going nowhere in life!'"

The packed studio audience were now all seated and very excited. I was to start the show with my normal introduction and then go into the hypnotic induction off-air – for the simple reason that if I presented a live hypnotic induction on TV, I could be held responsible for lots of TV viewers hypnotised in their own homes, and the consequences could be dire. The whole thing went like clockwork. Within minutes, I had twelve subjects all hypnotised, but I now had to place them back into the audience ("on ice", so to speak) and wait a considerable time before the live show started.

I was told that even the people that didn't like *Xarabank* as a programme watched this show and the ratings went through the roof. Overnight, I was a **"Hypnotic Star"**, (the title of my first book), a new household name in Malta, and all thanks to the marvellous Marcette.

The *Xarabank* show was a huge success and the Maltese press gave me rave reviews. *Razzett tal - Hbiberija* was now firmly placed on the map. Due to the hard work of Marcette, Nathan Farrugia, Razzett tal - Hbiberija's general manager, Peppi, PJ, John Paul and myself, many thousands of Maltese lira were raised that evening. The following night's show was sold out in advance and was wonderfully received. I was immediately invited back in three weeks' time to pre-record a lot of material for new shows that were to include "Hyp on the Street", so my next few days – which I had thought were to be spent relaxing and sunbathing were just the opposite – spent instead with meeting after meeting after meeting.

After discussions on how to raise more funds for *Razzett tal – Hbiberija,* it was decided that I would undertake once again my "being buried alive in a coffin". I knew I could do it due to my past exploits in England, but there are always risks attached to this sort of activity. The date was set but this time it would be conducted on a much grander scale. Marcette rapidly put in place everything that was requested in a most professional manner, assisted by her brother, Tonio, who ensured that the safety and logistics were in place. *Xarabank* covered the event and we tied it into another TV programme, but other Maltese channels and news media were also engaged.

Buried alive in Malta for charity, and (below) exhumed from the grave

A lot of my fans gathered to witness the committal and I was buried very deep in the ground in Marsascala. Unlike my previous "pauper's burial", this time I had the dignity of a granite headstone and a full nation of worshipers! I need not have worried – I had full back up on site with the emergency services present, including the

Author with Marcy and the President of Malta

fire service, doctors, National Guard, and, of course, the press.

I was exhumed in the evening as was the plan and all the "mourners" had returned to witness my resurrection. As I was removed from the cold bosom of the earth, I received lots of attention from the doctors checking my stats – hydration levels, pulse, etc. My first answer to the live TV news presenter was, "I now know what it feels like when someone has walked on your grave!"

After two successful seminars to help people stop smoking and lose weight, I mentioned to Jean Paul that I would like to meet the President of Malta. He looked at me seriously and replied, "Would you really? Leave it with me. He is my friend and I will speak to him." Two hours later I received a message: "The President will receive you at the Presidential Palace, Saint George's Square in Valetta, at one o'clock the following day." I was elated. I was going to meet His Excellency, Guido Demarco, the President of Malta.[1]

Marcette picked me up at the pre-arranged time and we drove into Valletta where we were to meet up with Jean Paul and his son, Jacques-Paul; we were to be received as a group, and as we entered the palace, Marcette looked at me with a large grin on her face and said, "Who would have believed that a general enquiry email to your agent in London would lead to us having afternoon tea with the President!" We were escorted to a room adjacent to the President's office and introduced to a member of the Special Forces who was assigned to protect the President. He then escorted us to the President where an aide performed the introductions. With a big beaming welcoming smile, the President shook hands with us, the official palace photographer taking several pictures.

President Guido Demarco was a very friendly and charming man. We chatted on several subjects. The President commented that he had been following my career in Malta and had watched my shows on television. After about twenty minutes, our time was up and it was time to leave. I was very proud to meet the President of Malta.

I returned several times to Malta over the following years, mainly for TV shows, but in 2012 Marcette suggested, due to my past success rate with my therapeutic work – namely, anti-smoking, weight loss control and phobias – that I return to Malta on a more regular basis. My Maltese fans, who loved me for my entertaining side, were now benefiting from something a lot more important, serious life changing issues.

After using my hypnotic skills for many years, I qualified as a UK registered hypnotherapist and received a distinction in my examinations. I have always had job satisfaction with everything I have done, especially on the stage, but now I was getting equally, if not more, satisfaction from helping people deal with problems, and to such a point on many occasions I have had to hold back emotion when witnessing the changes in people's lives.

I had now made several good friendships in Malta and I was invited to some very good *soirees,* including a lovely invitation from my good friend, Jacqueline Giordmaina, to attend "The President's August Moon Ball Party", in 2014. It was such a grand affair.

I often quote from the Chinese teacher and philosopher Confucius, who was born 551 BC:

"Find a job that you really love and you will never have to work a day in your life"!

I have always found this quotation to be very true and liberating. I am very lucky. I love the work I do.

In the next chapter, "Hypnosis & Therapy", I explain the fundamentals of hypnosis and try to explain, in my way, what it is that I am doing, with examples of treatments that have worked and enabled people to reach a better quality of life.

[1] *I was sad to receive the news that on 12th August, 2010, His Excellency, President Guido Demarco, passed away.*

CHAPTER ELEVEN
HYPNOSIS AND THERAPY

In this chapter, I explain how I perceive what hypnosis is – and there are various descriptions and ideas of hypnosis out there – and coming from that, how to induce a hypnotic state of mind. I also give examples of the treatment, experiences and results, and then present a "Q&A" checklist that will be useful preparation for anyone with an appointment with a hypnotherapist. I must stress the moral code at all times is strict client confidentiality.

The client always has to feel safe for the process to work well, and for this the client must be able to completely trust that what is a very private experience between us stays that way – completely private. So I will talk here about cases in only a general way. That way we can share what it is to be human – and that is a fascinating aspect of the work – but never mention people by name or any identifying details. Having said that, it is still very rare when a client does come to see me with a psychological issue that I have not already encountered, usually many times before. But when it does, it captivates me.

During my thirty years in this profession, I have gained a considerable amount of practical knowledge, and upon reading this book – and, particularly, this chapter – I hope you may become more enlightened in a subject that, at one time, was considered a mysterious "grey area". It is my intention to explain that away in down-to-earth "layman's terms".

I will not be delving into the history of hypnosis nor into the many famous historical and inspirational psychologists, such as Franz Anton Mesmer (1734-1815), Braid, Charcot, Freud, Erickson, etc. It is Mesmer who we attribute with drawing society's attention to the subject, hence the expression, "to be *mesmerised*". There is much confusion as to just what Mesmer practised but a great number of people from all walks of life were helped by him. Since his time, there are simply countless numbers of psychologists, far too many to be named here, but I thank their ground-breaking work which gave us a more sympathetic understanding of the subject. For the reader that would like to learn more on the history of hypnosis and psychology, the tools of the internet will answer all of your research questions, curiosity, and much, much more.

By this chapter in the book, you should now have a much better understanding on how I got to this stage in life. As a fun-loving adventurer, and very often a crazy person, this chapter represents a change in tack, adopting as it does a more serious vein.

What is Hypnosis?

Science simply cannot agree on what it is and how it works, although, as The British Society of Clinical Hypnosis states: "In therapy, hypnosis usually involves the person experiencing a sense of deep relaxation with their attention narrowed down, and focused on appropriate suggestions made by the therapist." These "suggestions" help people make positive changes within themselves. Long gone are the days when hypnosis was seen as waving a watch and controlling a person's mind. In a modern hypnotherapy session, clients are always aware and in control of the process, and it is generally accepted that all hypnosis is self-hypnosis. A hypnotist merely helps to facilitate and induce the trance state.

Contrary to popular belief, hypnosis is not a state of deep sleep. I describe it to my therapy clients like watching TV late at night while being very tired. When your eyes start closing, you desperately try to keep them open, to continue to watch TV. At this stage you are not asleep, but you are not awake either. It sounds paradoxical, but in fact you are in the transitional process of falling asleep. I will give you an analogy here: when an aircraft is on the runway ready for take-off, the datum point between being on the ground and becoming airborne is very similar in nature to being awake and ready for sleep. The process involves an enhanced state of awareness, concentrating entirely on my voice and the relaxing music which I play through a computer via a set of comfortable headphones.

In this state, the conscious mind is suppressed, or bridged, and the subconscious mind is revealed. I am then able to suggest ideas, concepts and lifestyle changes to the client, the suggestions of which become embedded, seeded, or planted, recorded deep in the fabric of the subconscious mind. Hypnotherapy aims to re-programme patterns of behaviour within the mind, enabling irrational fears, phobias, negative thoughts and suppressed emotions to be permanently overcome. In today's world, the most common treatments are for smoking cessation, weight loss and stress, but later in the chapter I will give examples of other issues where hypnosis has been able to achieve great results.

As the mind and body are released from conscious control during the relaxed trance-like state of hypnosis, breathing becomes slower and deeper, the pulse rate drops and the metabolic rate falls.

It is my belief that hypnosis works by altering the state of consciousness in such a way that the analytical left-hand side of the brain is turned off, while the non-analytical right-hand side is made more alert. The conscious control of the mind is inhibited, and the subconscious mind awoken. Since the subconscious mind is a deeper-seated, more instinctive force than the conscious mind, this is the part which has to change for the client's behaviour and physical state to alter. Unlike the conscious mind, the subconscious never switches off. It is active before you are born and ends only upon the death of the physical body. The subconscious deals with your dream states, bodily functions, habits, addictions and so much more. Such is the importance of this part of the mind.

For example, a client who consciously wants to overcome their fear of cockroaches may try everything they consciously can, but it will still fail as long as their subconscious mind retains this fear and prevents the patient from succeeding. Progress can only be made by reprogramming the subconscious so that deep-seated instincts and beliefs are removed or altered. I can succeed in this manner by using regression and suggestive therapy. If you will for a moment just allow yourself to think about this, you can visualise while you read. Travel back in time, to an important place in your memory – to when you started school for example, or work, or to your wedding day. Just pick any one of them and take yourself back. Right back. And when you are there, remember just one thing that happened. If you will, actually allow yourself to go there, see the place again as it was. Hear it all around you. Give yourself a long moment to soak it in, so you can almost touch it.

Reader, if you are one of the ones who can focus themselves in this way you are in effect a time traveller. With hypnotherapy, I can guide you back in time using the power of your mind and memory, to the source and core of any issue, and remove the negative emotions and associations, and break the link between the past's suppressed experiences and the present day.

How Do I get a Client into a State of Hypnosis?

Firstly, any misconceptions a client may have about hypnosis should be dispelled. The very reason that a client has come to see me in the first place indicates they want to change some behavioural habit or addiction. They have to want the treatment to work and a good rapport between the client and myself is not just important but essential. Keeping eye to eye contact at all times is also very important, up to the point he or she closes their eyes for the start of the hypnosis.

I always give a full explanation, as described above, but it is just as important to listen to everything the client tells me. In doing so, I am able to build up a client profile and we are then able to mutually agree on exactly what needs to change and in what direction to approach the issue.

My technique does not involve the client being put into a very deep sleep, and the client cannot be made to do anything they would not ordinarily do. They remain in control but share that control with me. And the client is always aware of their surroundings and situation.

I then start my induction with relaxing music and guide the client down into a deep state of hypnosis. When this is achieved, I work on the client's subconscious mind to deal with the issues discussed. Once completed, I slowly wake the client and the suggestions that I have given under hypnosis have now become *active* post hypnotic suggestions that work for the client during their daily waking hours in a natural, automatic way.

Hypnotherapists do differ in their technique. However, the *"POSITIVE RESULT"* is the most important part of our work. I am no different to any other professional person in that I need to be able to get satisfactory results for my clients, and when the client is really happy it also gives me great job satisfaction.

The Difference between Stage Comedy and Therapy

The state of hypnosis induced in the mind of a subject, in my view, is the same, whether the purpose is for entertaining on stage or used in a therapeutic way. There are different depths within the trance state, but the client does not necessarily need to go into a deep trance in therapy to receive benefit. However, for stage purposes, it is essential. The induction method is also very different.

When working the stage, I need to be able to find about twelve subjects who are very susceptible to hypnosis very quickly. I identify them by a simple hand locking experiment and the people that experience the hand lock sensation – fingers fixed and unable to move – prove to me that they are susceptible to a quick hypnotic induction. I then invite these willing volunteers to

179

the stage. For a public demonstration in the UK, volunteers need to be 18 years or over. However, if it is not in a public place – say, a house party – there is no age restriction. It is interesting here to note that most therapeutic hypnotherapists have contempt for stage hypnotists for various reasons. One of the main reasons, I believe, is that they think stage performers give hypnosis a bad name. I am fortunate to be able to see both sides of this viewpoint and the truly experienced professional hypnotist / entertainer will have the ability to wear both hats.

An organisation was formed many years ago by professional stage hypnotists in the UK, named FESH (the Federation of Ethical Stage Hypnotists). The remit was to unite fellow professionals

to promulgate the ethics of the profession and also to deal with an Act of Parliament in 1952, set up to regulate stage hypnosis. And since then, FESH has assisted with local authorities in giving advice in licencing matters. I am a long

Small therapy group session

standing senior committee member of this organisation and also a member of the Professional Hypnotherapy Practitioners Association.

Why Hypnotherapy?

If you are physically not well, you will go to see your doctor and hopefully he or she will give you medication or direct you to a specialist department to deal with your ailment. If you are unwell with a psychological problem, you may be referred to a psychologist, psychiatrist, psychotherapist or a hypnotherapist.

Within that sphere of treatment, you may receive medication to balance a chemical imbalance, cognitive behavioural therapy and other more direct and natural options of treatment, including hypnotherapy. Although drug treatments can be very effective, it is very important to take advice from your doctor on all matters concerning your health. But people are also waking up nowadays to the possibility of relief via alternative, less intrusive therapies.

However, hypnotherapy is completely and totally natural, which is why more and more people are trying it. I say daily to people that it is not a magic wand, and it will not work for everyone, and yes, some people will be disappointed, but you don't know that until you try it. And, for example, in trying to give up smoking, there are no guarantees that acupuncture, patches, medication or good old willpower will work for you either. And as an ex-smoker I have the experience to know what it is like. I gave up smoking cigarettes seventeen years ago and it is one of the best things I have ever done. Smoking cessation is one of the most common requests from my clients and – to my great pleasure, reader – I have stopped thousands of people worldwide. Now, that's a fact! Politicians, neurosurgeons, bank managers, famous artists, priests, celebrities, CEOs, police officers, lawyers, and folk from all different walks of life rank amongst my most positive statistic.

Likewise, obesity is a major problem in the western world, and not only is it a big health issue, it is costing health services billions annually – and it is mainly, but not always, self-generated. By retraining your mind with hypnotherapy to reduce the portions of food you eat, monitoring carbohydrate levels, removing the sweet tooth, stopping snacking and comfort eating, and generating motivation for gentle vascular exercise, you will enable yourself to reduce weight over a period of time. By losing weight, your self-esteem and confidence will improve, and it will help you to achieve a greater balance. We all like to look and feel good – it is a part of being human.

The good news is that I offer a service that can assist with most of these issues and more. I always say, do not suffer in silence if you have a problem, talk about it, and do something to fix it. There is a limit to what hypnosis can cure, people that are seriously mentally ill with delusional personality disorders are better treated in another manner.

I have on several occasions assisted people that have been suicidal. Whenever I confront this situation with a client, all my alarm bells will ring. The wellbeing of a client is of *paramount importance* and when I have been asked to help in these matters it takes priority over everything else that I am doing – and there is *no exception* to that. It is a sad statistic of this modern world that we all know and have loved some souls who have taken their own lives. One of the most rewarding things that brings job satisfaction to it highest level is when a client makes contact months after treatment and says, "Thanks for saving my life." This has happened to me on several occasions and it always brings me to tears, it really does. If it didn't, I wouldn't be human. I have experienced this on a personal level because I said the same to the surgeon that saved my life many years earlier. I tried to get eye-to-eye contact with him from my hospital bed but he would not give it – he did not need to – I just knew how he felt.

Therapy Cases

As I said at the beginning of this chapter, confidentiality is of paramount importance when dealing with any client. A bond of mutual trust and respect needs to be given and received by both therapist and client.

The examples of cases that I give below range from what you may consider strange to bizarre. But, I assure you that all are true. These examples are intended to provide you with the diverse range of issues for which clients seek hypnotherapy, and I hope this highlights the message once again that if you are troubled, and no matter what the issue is, do not suffer in silence – speak up, get help. The identities of the clients involved are shielded; I see many people and practise in several countries, so if I have treated you for a similar issue, it does not necessarily refer to your particular case individually. As in several circumstances, they are also not a one-off examples, as I will have treated many similar cases, and all names and specific details have been changed. This is intended to bring about awareness of how we are all so different and unique in our own special ways, and how hypnosis can help us retrain our thoughts and actions and bring about a positive result. It also demonstrates that hypnotherapy is not just used to assist smokers to kick the habit, for people to lose weight, or for the reduction of stress and anxiety, but it is also successful for many different, severe, and sometimes life threatening, issues.

Working and getting results with children is also very rewarding. The youngest child that I have helped with therapy was just nine years old. A different and more imaginative induction and method is required to work with young children.

I had the pleasure just last year of removing an intense phobia of birds, in particular pigeons, from a ten year old girl, that I shall name "Jacey", which had developed five years earlier, while Jacey was celebrating her fifth birthday with friends and family. A clown was employed to entertain the children, and during the entertainment the clown produced a pigeon from out of his sleeve, and as it emerged it flew hard and fast straight into young Jacey's face. It was such a shock to the system it took the parents quite a while to calm her down. And from that day, Jacey developed an intense fear of all birds, and especially pigeons, as you can understand. This fear grew stronger and to such a point that whenever she went out of her home, her subconscious "pigeon radar" was activated. A trip out to the city became impossible due to this fear. Jacey, now ten, came to see me with her parents. She was a lovely young girl and after a one hour session I managed to completely remove all traces of the negative emotion and fear. A few days later I heard via social media that she was a totally different person and had already travelled into the city. I was

183

also thanked not only by her parents but by her uncles and aunts as well. It was a good result, but it is worth noting that Jacey had previously suffered five years of unnecessary hell before she was brought to see me.

It is impossible to remember every client's therapy session and it is also important that the therapist knows how to let go of a client's emotions after the session for the wellbeing of the therapist. However, I am human and from time to time I also hold on to sad feelings when I witness a person's suffering. The following case involves a pretty young lady aged 18 who came to visit me. I have named her "Lyndsey".

Lyndsey's parents had basically abandoned her at the age of sixteen. Her mother had left the country and her father was in a new relationship and didn't want to know her any more. So, for the last two years she had been virtually homeless. She spoke well and was an intelligent girl, but, in the necessity of circumstance, she took the shelter of a young man and moved in with him and his father.

As the weeks passed by, while her boyfriend was out at work, the father forced Lyndsey to have sex with him on a very regular, almost daily, basis. He informed her that, if she told anybody, she would be thrown out of the house. Poor Lyndsey was in a terrible state of mind. She had real issues with guilt, but if she was put out onto the street, where would she go? She would be destitute. Lyndsey had nobody to talk to and I was feeling her sadness. She had eventually broken up with her boyfriend and soon enough she had found another man and had moved into his home. In my office, she broke down and cried uncontrollably at the grief and emotion she was suffering from the actions of her ex's father. I managed to treat Lyndsey, to calm her down and eventually help her deal with the emotional after effects. A few months afterwards, a message was passed to me that she had fully overcome her bad experiences.

And it did not end here. At the end of the session, she told me she was pregnant and that she was still smoking more than a packet of cigarettes each day, and her partner likewise. Of course, I gave her a lecture on the importance of giving up while she was carrying a child. Then, to back the lecture up, I invited both Lyndsey and her partner, free of charge, to visit me the following week. Sadly, they did not show. Worried about her, and now also for the baby, I wrote to the last known address given to me. I purchased a lot of baby clothes and equipment that I wanted them to have as a gift, but sadly she was not at this address. Perhaps smoking was something she clung to, maybe I had overplayed its importance. I don't know whatever became of Lyndsey, but having young daughters of my own it makes me sad to think.

And, thank goodness, not all cases are negative. Sometimes I receive bizarre requests. One day I had a man who came to see me say, "Look, Mr. Bates, I will cut out the unnecessary small talk. I am a drug dealer and I have recently tested and bought a large quantity of very potent cocaine, and, afterwards, I was so high that I hid the drugs and now I cannot find them!" I sat looking at him with my mouth wide open. I had to explain to him – diplomatically, as he was a very big bloke – that, unfortunately, I would not be able to help him find his drugs. He left very frustrated.

Reader, you may or may not be surprised to hear that a lot of people suffer with sexual problems. Listening to clients' problems with their sex lives to me is no shock or surprise – I have heard it all before, or, at least, most of it. Five years ago, I had a pleasant middle aged couple come to visit me. Their problem was that the wife would get drunk each and every night and beat the living hell out of her husband, then not remember a thing the next day. They still loved each other but badly needed this alcoholic nightmare to go away. In these types of cases, I would, under hypnosis, ease the quantity of alcohol down, gradually, over a period of time, to avoid withdrawal symptoms ("cold turkey") and deal with it gently. After explaining this to my clients, I was asked to forget this procedure and, if the treatment was successful, then she was prepared to face the demons. Under the circumstances, and after a further explanation, I agreed to continue in the manner that the three of us had discussed.

Two months later they revisited me. They came into my office holding hands with a smile on their faces. I was delighted to hear that the therapy had worked 100%, but when I asked what I could do for them now, the lady's head dropped and all eye to eye contact was lost. I knew immediately what it was but I kindly waited. The husband took control over the conversation and said, "Since the alcohol problem is now controlled, she has completely lost all her sex drive." Since I knew she was very susceptible to hypnosis, after another deep session I now hope, and expect, that the couple are having a "blissfully" happy, loving and sexual relationship!

Removing a horse phobia live on TVM

In 2014, I was back on a regular TV show, helping people with all sorts of problems, including phobias with cockroaches, horses, needles, dogs, mice and, believe it or not, king prawns. One part of this programme involved working with a sixty year old man who had a severe problem with claustrophobia. For years this fear had created lots of embarrassment and inconvenience in his life, and it was his turn to have my fascinated attention. In a very short time, using my skills deep within his subconscious mind, I took away this insecurity and fear, but it was now time to put it to the test. We left the studio with the camera crew and went to a local hotel. In his own time I patiently suggested for him to enter the lift and press the button. He was very apprehensive at first but after a few minutes he entered with all our crew in tally. He pressed the button for the 9th floor and away we went. He burst out crying genuine tears of relief, recorded for TV and all to see. It was a great experience for us, and even the cameraman could see the joy on this man's face. It didn't stop there, though – he went up and down, up and down. We couldn't get him out in the end.

One year previously, I had dealt with another client with a very similar phobia. However, not only was my client claustrophobic, but also agoraphobic. This condition had prevented this particular elderly client from leaving her home; she had been trapped there for almost thirty years! Her daughter had escorted her to my office and, by using the stairs and not the lift – and with a lot of cajoling – they had made their way up to see me. I was shocked to hear that the journey that day was one of only a handful of times she had left her home in many, many years. I knew just how important this session was to her. My client desperately believed in me and I was, as always, going to give her my 100% best. She was, luckily, very, very susceptible, and within the hour we were ready to put our session result into practise.

I took her by the arm and escorted her to the nearest lift. I called the lift and it arrived in seconds. "Are you ready?" I asked. She nodded and, holding her hand, we both entered. I instructed her to press the button for the ground floor and, with a shaking hand, she slowly did. By the time we reached the ground floor, the smile on her face was of pure pleasure. It doesn't end there, though; I walked her out of the lobby and into the sunshine where she took my hand again – and we danced in the street! She was shouting to the pedestrians in the street, "I am free, I am free!" It must have looked comical, but this was seriously a very important moment in this lady's life. After big hugs, and more big hugs, the lady departed with her daughter, big smiles on everyone's faces, including mine.

Having a rapport with a client, as I have stated previously, is very important. The following session ended in a manner that the client would never have dreamed. I am also sure that not many other therapists or professional hypnotists would have had the courage to do what I did.

I will name my client "Neil". Neil was a twenty four year old, tall and thinly built, rather reserved young man. Neil had come to see me with a condition called "shy bladder". The condition is not uncommon and I had treated three similar clients previously. Neil had a psychological block which prevented him from going to the toilet "for a wee" in public and he had to plan his day accordingly as to when he takes fluids. Whenever he was in a public toilet and looking to empty his bladder, he would simply freeze if another customer entered, and he would have to walk out quickly. Even when out socially, he would have to basically plan ahead for every "piddling" eventuality. Just imagine how terrible a problem this must be.

After explaining the process and preparing him for therapy, it transpired he was very susceptible to hypnosis and allowed me in to his subconscious. On this occasion,

Removing flight phobia

I used regression therapy to try and find out how and why this started as, consciously, Neil did not know any reasons for his problem, and it had been this way for many years. He had got used to it, as humans are creatures of habit, and we have the ability to adapt and adjust to what is needed.

During the regression, I escorted him deep within his memory, back in time to his former years, back to being seven years old. I was very fortunate as I uncovered a memory that he had long forgotten, a memory of him in a public toilet on his own, when a man, obviously a paedophile, was blatantly watching him urinate. This negative memory was suppressed and long forgotten on a conscious level, but this was the root cause of his problem. I managed to remove these negative memories and remove the link from the past to the present and then gave him positive suggestion to enable him to go into public toilets without fear, like any other male.

Upon awaking him, and after a glass of water and a final talk, I escorted him out of my office, instructing him to follow. "Where are we going?" he asked. "To the toilet," I replied, "for a pee." He followed me in – I am sure apprehensively – but we stood side by side at the urinal in a public toilet, and we both emptied our bladders!

My final example of therapy in this book was that which I gave to a man who had led a very sad life indeed, and I will never forget him. I shall call him "Tom". Several years ago, I was ten minutes away from my call time on the set of a TV programme and the late invited audience guests were quickly ushered by security to their seats. I was out of the green room and in the wings, fully miked up, psyched up, and ready to go. I noticed a man that was following me with parallel steps on the other side of the security barrier. I held eye contact with him and he moved out of sight of security, though still following step for step. Alarm bells rang in my head and so I contacted security and asked them to carefully watch this man as there was something out of place and not quite right.

With moments away from my introduction to the show, I thought, "Sod it. I need to settle this before I go to work." So I crossed the barrier, not knowing what confrontation I may be heading into. Upon reaching this stranger, I said to him, "Are you ok?" His demeanour changed the moment I spoke to him. I was so wired and alert that I literally felt one step ahead of everything, and I just knew this man was not a threat. He had come to the TV show by invitation, but hoping also that I may be able to help him. He told me he was desperate to have his phobia of dentist work removed. He told me that his teeth were rotten and he was in continual pain twenty four hours a day. I reassured him that I would help him as soon as possible even though my diary was full for weeks ahead. My manager was at hand and passed on a business card to him when he said, "Mr. Bates, I have another problem. I am destitute and have no money." I could see in the manner of his attire he was telling me the truth. I replied, "What do you need money for?" He looked at me strangely, and I said, "You don't need money to come to see me, and further still, I am going to make an appointment for you to see me first thing in the morning!" Tom had tears in his eyes. I don't think anybody had offered him any kindness in a long time.

The next day Tom arrived and presented me with a hand-written life story, all on a single piece of paper. I will not divulge the content as it was very private but all I can say is that I was so, so glad he came to see me.

I once watched Bill Gates – the richest man in the world – say on TV, "Life is not fair," and do you know what? He is not wrong.

I mentioned earlier that clients with mental problems may need to be treated in a different manner. Across the other end of the scales, we have the criminally insane, both male and female. Here, we enter the world of patients whose minds are wired differently to the majority of the human race. My visit to the high security psychiatric hospital, Broadmoor, further enlightened me, providing a greater understanding of the mind. At this point in the chapter, I would like to share with you my visit behind the closed doors of Broadmoor.

Broadmoor and the Yorkshire Ripper

Broadmoor Hospital is a specialist service that provides assessment, treatment and care in conditions of high security for men. It is in Crowthorne, West Berkshire. It first opened its doors to male patients as a lunatic asylum in 1864 and it is one of three high-security psychiatric hospitals in England. They treat people with mental illness and personality disorders who represent a high degree of risk to themselves or to others by using a combination of medication and psychological therapies. So when an invitation was offered to visit this place, I instantly accepted without a further thought.

I had a therapist friend who worked part time at the hospital and he arranged for me to have a guided group tour which included a building tour, lecture on financial structures and an opportunity to talk with the patients. As you would hope and expect, the security is very high.

During our guided tour, we were encouraged to talk to the patients if they wanted to talk to us. It was spelt out to us *not* to discuss their case histories or medication. To all intents and purposes, these patients looked absolutely no different to anybody else that you may see in a shop, on a bus or

Broadmoor, home of the Yorkshire Ripper

at your place of work. Which is perhaps a bit scary. We were then told not to be fooled as they could be very, very dangerous. It was also interesting to see that all the staff throughout the hospital had their backs to the wall for security purposes. It was also a thought-provoking observation that the staff were always alert to what was happening in the peripheral.

I instigated a conversation with the most notorious high profile psychopath in British history, Peter Sutcliffe, "The Yorkshire Ripper". Sutcliffe was found guilty of the murder of thirteen women and of attempting to murder seven others. As I just stated, he looked no different to the next guy on the street and our conversation was very brief. Sutcliffe has been the target of several assaults over the years. In 1996, 1997 and 2007, he was attacked, causing facial injury and, in one incident, the loss of an eye.

Among some of the other notorious killers with whom we chatted was Ronnie Kray, the infamous gangland killer from London (now deceased), and another patient who killed his mother and then ate her. We were warned to be on our guard at all times as even when you are having an interesting conversation and you feel the rapport is going well you never know when their psychopathic mind will turn against you, for while you are in there you are always at your peril.

I end this experience at Broadmoor with something to make you think. According to the media, one in every one hundred people living in the UK has the potential to develop psychopathic tendencies. It's a scary thought!

The questions and answers listed below are the most frequently asked questions that I receive and can act as a checklist, should you wish to see me or another hypnotherapist for a consultation. Each therapist uses their own methods but in general this guide below should answer most questions that you may have and prepare you for hypnosis. Remember, "Do not suffer in silence, and do get help!"

Questions and Answers – What You Need to Know Before a Session of Hypnosis

What is hypnosis?

Hypnosis is an altered state of awareness. It is a very special tool which forms a bridge between the conscious and subconscious mind. In this state, the positive suggestions can reach your subconscious mind while the conscious mind remains relaxed. You will find that suggestions which have been given to you in hypnosis will resurface in your conscious thinking mind after your session, and these will be the thoughts that produce changes in your behaviour or your way of thinking and feeling.

When I am "under" will I be asleep?

To be hypnotised is like being in a pleasantly relaxed and drowsy state. You will be aware of everything that is happening and what is being said to you the whole time. If you are attending for several sessions of hypnotherapy, you may find that you drift a little deeper on each occasion. However, you will still be aware of everything around you and of what is being said. If there were an emergency during the therapy session, you would immediately be fully awake and in complete control of your senses and your reactions.

What can I expect at the hypnotherapy session and how long will it last?

The hypnotist will probably spend a good deal of time just talking to you before actually hypnotising you. This discussion time is important in order for you to talk about your problems and also to set your mind at rest about any aspect that bothers you. Please allocate one hour for your appointment. It's best to arrive 10 minutes prior to your appointment.

How do I know I will wake up from hypnosis?

No-one has ever remained in hypnosis indefinitely. If anything were to happen to your therapist or if you stopped listening to a hypnotic CD part way through, you would merely progress from a hypnotic state into a light sleep, and then gently wake up naturally 10-20 minutes later, with no ill effects.

Are there any side effects from hypnosis?

The only side effects are the beneficial ones of feeling more relaxed afterwards and feeling more positive about whatever it was you sought hypnotherapy for. Hypnosis is a perfectly natural state.

How many sessions will I need?

This is a difficult question to answer. I have had many smokers who have stopped completely after having only one hypnotherapy session with me, and I have also cured many people of their phobias again in only one session. However, not

193

l people are the same and sometimes a person may need several sessions for an issue to be dealt with and resolved.

Can I eat and drink beforehand?

Eating and drinking in moderation beforehand will not affect the hypnotic session. It is better, however, not to consume a huge meal beforehand because the possible feelings of discomfort might impede your ability to relax. Equally, you should not be hungry as this too could cause distractions for you. Please do not have alcohol or caffeine before your hypnotherapy appointment. It is also important that you do not have a full bladder before a session.

What clothes should I wear?

The keyword here is "comfort". The more comfortable you are, the easier it will be for you to relax. It is NOT advisable therefore to wear garments that are very restricting or too tight, nor should you wear shoes that pinch. I always advise clients to feel free to remove their shoes so that they can relax more.

Can anyone be hypnotised?

With few exceptions, anyone who wants to be hypnotised can be. The opposite is also true – if you do NOT want to be hypnotised you will not be. It is therefore important that there is trust and co-operation between yourself and the hypnotist, as this will help the hypnotherapy to be successful.

Is hypnotherapy suitable for everyone?

Someone with a history of epilepsy should not be hypnotised. Even if the situation is under control with drugs, the altered state could actually (but not necessarily) induce an epileptic fit. Clients with a drink or drug addiction are advised to ask their doctor for permission / referral before being treated by hypnosis. It is important that there be a good mutual understanding of the language in which the therapy will be conducted.

Can I bring someone with me?

You are very welcome to bring a family member or friend with you to any of my sessions. Please advise in advance if you require a member of our staff to be present during the hypnosis treatment.

CHAPTER TWELVE
FOR MY FUTURE GENERATIONS

On 2nd April, 2002, I woke out of a deep sleep at around 3.00 a.m. with the overwhelming desire to write this poem below, especially for you, my family, and my future generations.

It was with a rush of adrenaline that I dashed to find a pen and paper before I would lose this inspiration. I don't know what will happen in the future but please always remember, you are "SPECIAL".

Life in general is not fair and you will learn this on your journey through it. The most important thing is to *"love and be happy"*.

Look after your (my) family and everybody you care for, be kind and thoughtful towards others. Treat all people with respect.

You will make mistakes on the way for sure, but learn by those mistakes, be a free thinker, **"own your own mind"** and don't become brainwashed with stupid ideology.

Nothing lasts forever so truly enjoy the moment and every waking minute. Time passes so quickly and, before you know it, it will be your time to depart the stage.

I have had more than my fair share of ups and downs. However, so far, I have lived a very fruitful and amazing life. It is my wish that you pass this book on to your own children so they can share my life's experiences.

Peace and love to you all, and always remember – I am only a thought away!

WITH DEVOTED LOVE TO MY FUTURE GENERATIONS

Through my veins runs blood sincere

When you need me call my name, I will be near

From generation to generation you are part of me

You always will be, you are part of me

From your infant birth to your last final breath,

When you need me, call my name, I will be near

Be honest, just and upright and you will have no fear.

Alan Bates, 2nd April, 2002.

For your information I have researched the ancient history of our surname.

The Ancient History of the Surname "Bates"

Of the Anglo-Saxon surnames of England, few are more distinguished than Bates. Now, the historical trail of this surname has emerged from the mists of time to become an influential surname in history.

In a careful professional research of such ancient manuscripts as the doomsday book compiled in 1086 A.D. by Duke William of Normandy, the Ragman Rolls (1291 – 1296), a record of homage rendered to King Edward 1st of England, the Curia Regis Rolls, the Pipe Rolls, the Hearth Rolls, parish registers, baptismal, tax records and other ancient documents researchers found the first mention of the name Bates in Yorkshire, where they had been seated from ancient times, long before the Norman conquest in 1066.

Many different spellings were founding the archives researched. Although my name Bates, occurred in many manuscripts, from time to time the surname was shown spelt as Bates, Batts, Bats, Bate, Bateson, Baits, Baites, Baytes, Bayte, and these variations

Atlanta, Dad, Jay, Estelle, Keira & Amber Bates

in spelling occurred within the history, even between father and son. There were many reasons for these spelling variations, some deliberate some accidental.

The Anglo Saxons were a fair skinned people who came to England about the year 400 led by General / Commanders Hengiest and Horsa. After 600 years rule of England the Norman invasion from France and their victory at the Battle of Hastings, the Normans have found many of the vanquished Saxon landowners to forfeit their land to Duke William and his invading Norman Nobles. The Saxons became oppressed under Norman rule, and some moved northward to the Midlands, Lancashire and Yorkshire, even into Scotland.

The family name Bates emerged as a notable English family name in the county of Yorkshire, where they settled in the East Riding. The name is a diminutive of Bartholomew. By the year

1200 they had moved north into Northumberland and Scotland to escape the oppression of the Norman overlords. Walter Bate rendered homage to King Edward I of England during his brief conquest of Scotland. He held estates in Lanarkshire. Robert Bates, of Spynie, was a minister of the gospel. In Northumberland their seat was at Millbourne Hall and Ovington Hall. Thomas Bates of Morpeth was a Member of Parliament and great friend of Queen Mary and Queen Elizabeth. For those interested in further research, I would recommend "Genealogies of the families of Bate and Kirkland of Ashby-De-La-Zouche" by J.P. Rylands, 1877. Notable amongst the family at this time was Thomas Bates of Morpeth.

During the 16th, 17th and 18th centuries England was ravaged by religious and political conflict. Puritanism, Catholicism, Royalist and parliamentary forces shed much blood. Many families were freely "encouraged" to migrate to Ireland, or to the "colonies".

In Ireland, settlers became known as the "adventurers for land in Ireland", where they undertook to maintain the protestant faith. Twenty-Two families of Bates were transferred into Ireland during the Plantation of Ulster.

The new world held many attractions for the adventurous. They sailed aboard overcrowded ships which were pestilence ridden, sometimes 30% to 40% of the passenger list never reached their destination, their numbers reduced by dysentery, cholera, small pox, typhoid or the elements.

Amongst the settlers which could be considered a kinsman of the surname Bates, or a variable spelling of that family name was Alice Bate who settled in New England in 1635; Clement Bate settled in Hingham, Mass in 1630; John Bate settled in Virginia in 1621; Leticia and William Bate settled in Barbados in 1680, with servants; James Bates, who settled in Boston, Mass in 1635; John Bates who settled in Virginia in 1623; Robert Bates who settled in Barbados in 1669; Dorothy Batts settled in Virginia in 1634; John Batts settled in New Jersey in 1677 with servants; Henry Bateson settled in Maryland in 1774: James and John

Bateson landed in Philadelphia, Pa in 1860; John Baites settled in Virginia in 1685. In Newfoundland, H.C. Bate settled in St John's in 1797; William Baitt settled in Trinity in 1798; Thomas Bates, was a planter of Twillingate in 1820; Thomas, from Clonmell, Tipperary, was married in St John's in 1821, and many more. There is a Bates Pond in Newfoundland.

The treacherous trek from the port of entry also claimed many victims as many joined the wagon trains to the prairies or to the west coast. During the American War of Independence, many loyalists to the Crown made their way north to Canada about 1790, and became known as the United Empire Loyalists.

More recent notables of this surname, Bates, include many distinguished persons, Sir Alfred Bates, Lawyer; General John Bates; Sir John Bates, Consul General, Australia; Allan Bates, Author (not me); Herbert Ernest Bates, Novelist, Author of "Fair Stood the Wind for France" and many more; Ven. Alban Bate, M.A., DCnL., Archdeacon of St. John, New Brunswick, retired; Hon. Mr. Justice Bate, senior Puisne Judge, High Court of Justice, Northern States of Nigeria; Sir Walter Edwin Bate, O.B.E., Barrister, solicitor and Notary Public, Hastings, New Zealand; Professor Walter Jackson Bate, Harvard University; Dame Zara Bate; Major General William Bate; Baron Deramore (Bateson); Andrew Bateson, Q.C.; Fredrick Wilse Bateson, English Literature, Oxford University; Air Vice Marshall Robert Norman Bateson; Rear Admiral Stuart Latham Bateson.

The research also determined the many Coats of Arms matriculated by the family name. The most ancient grant of a coat of Arms found was; three silver right hands on a black background. The crest is, a naked man holding a willow wand.

The ancient family motto for my name is; **"Et Manu Et Corde"** translated means "by hand and by heart".

CHAPTER THIRTEEN
MEETING OF SOULS

I would like to acknowledge and also thank my family, friends, colleagues and associates, named below in alphabetical order, for their love, friendship, help and guidance. It does not matter if we only met very briefly nor if we have lifelong attachment; combined with the laws of chaos, the universe has brought us together, our paths have crossed, and our souls have touched.

The analogy below, I believe, is a superb way of prioritising your life. So, love the people who treat you right and forget about the ones who don't!

ANALOGY OF LIFE'S PRIORITY

When things in your life seem almost too much to handle, when 24 hours in a day are not enough, remember what I am about to tell you now – the mayonnaise jar and the two beers.

A professor stood before his philosophy class with several items in front of him. When the class began, he wordlessly picked up a very large and empty mayonnaise jar and proceeded to fill it with golf balls. He then asked the students if the jar was full. They all agreed that it was.

The professor then picked up a box of pebbles and poured them into the jar. He shook the jar lightly and the pebbles rolled into the open areas between the golf balls. He then asked the students again if the jar was full, and they agreed it was.

The professor next picked up a box of sand and poured it into the jar. Of course, the sand filled up everything else. He asked once more if the jar was full, the students responded with a unanimous, "Yes".

The professor then produced two beers from under the table and poured the entire contents into the jar, effectively filling the empty space between the sand, to the students' amusement.

"Now," said the professor, as the laughter subsided, "I want you to recognize that this jar represents your life. The golf balls are the important things; your family, your children, your health, your friends and your favourite passions, and if everything else was lost and only the balls remained, your life would still be full. The pebbles are the other things that matter like your job, your house and your car. The sand is everything else, the small stuff."

"If you put the sand into the jar first," he continued, "there is no room for the pebbles or the golf balls. The same goes for life. If you spend all your time and energy on the small stuff, you will never have room for the things that are most important to you.

Pay attention to the things that are critical to your happiness. Spend time with your children. Spend time with your parents. Visit your grandparents. Take your partner out to dinner, there will always be time to clean the house and mow the lawn. Take care of the golf balls first, the things that really matter. Set your priorities – the rest is just sand."

One of the students raised her hand and inquired what the beer represented.

The professor smiled and said, "I'm glad you asked. The beer just shows you that no matter how full your life may seem, there's always room for a couple of beers with a friend."

You have a namecheck here because you have played a part of some description in my life. The life we live should be valued, cherished, enjoyed, and lived "to the max." If you are reading this and have played a part in my life but do not have a namecheck here, you are no less valued.

Key: (f) Immediate family (d) Deceased

A

Aaron & Keira Thompson
Aaron & Michelle Micallef (Malta)
Adam Coburn
Adam Night
Adam, Harry & Becky Roberts (f)
Adrian Catterall
Adrian Houghton (Singapore)
Agnes Melles (Hungary)
Agnes Raese (USA)
Aimee Wood (Malta)
Alan & Debbie Moore
Alan Cooper
Alan Kettal
Alan Knott
Alan Mail
Alan Owen
Alan Trigg (f) (d)
Alan Tuohey
Alan Williams (USA)
Alan, Paul & Margi Morgan
Alastair Macintyre (d)
Albert Anyon
Alex & Karen Wilson
Alex Fabry (Bali)
Alice Boughey (d)
Alnifa Hackney (USA)
Alternative Radio
Aly & Lara Goodchild
Amanda Buckley
Amber Bondin (Malta)
Amber Elizabeth Bates (f)
Andre King (New Zealand)
Andrea Boardman
Andrew Toth (Hungary)
Andy & Michael Gould

Andy & Steve Garry
Andy & Wahyuningsih Walsh (Bali)
Andy Black
Andy Butcher
Andy Christian
Andy Dunlop
Andy Georgiou (Cyprus)
Andy Goodfellow
Andy Matthews (Ibiza)
Andy Smith
Andy Wright
Angela Borg (Malta)
Angela Cardus Murray
Angela Ferns Clarke
Angela Read
Angelo Xuereb (Malta)
Ann & Lynn Monkhouse
Ann Roberts Challinor
Ann Young
Anna & Nick Harrison, Coughlan
Anne & Gary Archer
Anne Millington
Annie Tarpey Poole (f) (d)
Anthony & Penny Peake
Anthony Jacko Jackson
Archie & Joyce Beggs
Argyle Miles (Australia)
Arthur Youd
Arthur, Bob & Joyce
Ashley & George Gatt (Malta)
Atlanta Bates (f)
Atlantic Associates
Atmosphere Birkenhead
B
Barron Brothers
Barry & Hillary Diamond

Barry Fallows
Barry Godwin
Barry Luke & Ansha Jones (Australia)
Barry Mac
Barry Massam
Barry Nichols
Basil Keys
Bentleys Mold
Bernard Green (d)
Bernice Robe Quinn
Bernie & Elizabeth (d) Doyle
Beth McGuiness
Bev Littler (d)
Bill & Ma'am Barclay (USA)
Bill & Zoe Chambers
Bill Crossley (d)
Bill Gannon (f) (d)
Bill Halewood (d)
Bill James
Bill Lawley
Billy & Dora Edwards
Billy Butler
Billy Fitch
Billy Gillbanks
Billy Johnson
Billy Jones
Billy Lewis
Billy Moore
Billy Nichols
Bob Kane
Bobby Laycock (d)
Bonkers show bars
Boogieland Entertainment
Bradley Bates (f)
Brendan O'Connell (Ireland)
Brendan Riley

Brendon Kerr
Brian & Ann Black
Brian & Shirley Johnson
Brian Anderson
Brian Capper
Brian Farrell
Brian Hart
Brian Hough
Brian Laycock
Brian Sault (d)

C

Callum Hall
Capt. Hugh & Jean Flanagan (d)
Carl & Mo Rosario
Caroline Jones (Spain)
Carol Jones
Carolyn Hughes
Cat & Chris Norris
Cathy Saunders
Cathy Stracquadaneo (USA)
Charles (DJC) Bull
Charles Bates (f) (d)
Charles Darwin (Jamaica)
Charles Portelli (Malta)
Charlie & Peter Copson
Charlie (Pope) Harris
Charlie Seely
Chase Lynch (USA)
Chris & Jill Sullivan
Chris Chapman
Chris Currie
Chris Fisher
Chris James
Chris Trigg
Chris, Wendy & Andy Goldstone
Christine Hamlett Walsh

Christine Watson
Claire Sweeney
Clare & Mark Fleming
Clare Xuereb (Malta)
Clayton Barbara (Malta)
Cliff Millinoski (USA)
Clo & George DaSilva
Clubland Entertainment
Colin & Sue McCombe
Colin & Val Tunstall
Colin Gordon
Colin Lewis
Colin Peckham (New Zealand)
Colin Rowlands
Colin, Leroy & Jean Mangon
Colonel Charles Halt (USA)
Cynthia Payne

D

D. J. Uncle Dunk
D.J. Jay
D.J. Jimmi Sea
Dame Joan Bakewell
Damien Finn
Daniel Morris (f)
Danny Black
Danny Morris
Darlene Iles (USA)
Darren Cragg
Darren Hibberd
Dasha Pisani (Malta)
Dave & Cat Graham
Dave & Corina Robinson
Dave & Ellie (d) Stewart
Dave & Lyn McCarthy
Dave & Pauline Owen
Dave (d) & Becky Davies

Dave Bladon
Dave Bradley
Dave Cole
Dave Darlington (Denmark)
Dave Doherty
Dave Kaye
Dave Morris (f)
Dave Ralph (USA)
Dave Roberts
Dave Rodgigious
Dave Symington
Dave Wakeham (Germany)
Dave Williams
Dave, Cam & Sue Toner
Davey T
David & Linda Nicholls
David & Lisa Snook
David & Margie Hughes
David & Val Seabridge
David Gauci (Malta)
David Millington
David Parry
David Picken
Dean Owen
Debbie Pond
Debbie Walker
Delavor (d)
Delia, Jo & Ged Sainsbury (NZL)
Demajo Dental (Malta)
Denise Lee
Dennis & Christine Morgan
Dennis Dickinson (CFI)
Dennis Hammer Sound
Dennis Soloman (d)
Derek & Gwen Acorah
Derek (d) & Dot Lamb

Derek Gordon
Derek, Jack & Anita Kaye
Des Mitchell
Des Wilkes
Desa Deary
Diane & Mike Ruddock
Diane and Colin Christian
Dianne Barlow
Don & Doris Andrews
Don & Jan Price J.P.
Don Biffel
Don Douglas
Don Woods
Donna Worthington
Donny Mackey (d)
Dorianne Camilleri (Malta)
Doris & Vic Henri
Dot & Walt (USA)
Douglas Fishbone (USA)
Dougy Bates
Dr Alan & Vi Roberts
Dr Ciaran Walsh
Dr Duncan (d)
Dr Jean Paul Demajo (Malta)
Dr Steve Jones
Dr, Sandy Cachia Zammit (Malta) (d)
DT & G

E

Eamonne Sadler (Indonesia)
Earl & Pauline Ayres (USA)
Edd Dillon
Eddie & Nicky Fitzpatrick
Eddie Burke
Eddie Cox (d)
Eddie Denmark
Eddie Jones

Eddie Lucas
Eddie Pagan
Edna & Steve Jones
Eileen Tai
Eleanor Pullicino (Malta)
Elsa Louise Todd
Eric (d) & Grace Knowles
Eric Nickson (d)
Eric Nuttall
Erica & Luca Case
Estelle Buckley Bates (f)
Esther Rantzsen
Euan Martin
Eve Korosi (Hungary)
F
Fabian Demicoli (Malta)
Fats Davis
FESH
Fogwell Flax
Frances Skyner (d)
Frank & Selina Maldon (f) (d)
Frank Darrah
Frank Line
Frankie Allen
Fredrick & Laine Hine
G
Gail & Duncan (Dubai)
Gary & Debbie Bates (f)
Gary & Jan Dawson
Gary & Laura Vost
Gary & Sheila Skyner
Gary Dakin
Gary Fox
Gary Joy
Gary Laycock
Gary O'Keefe

Gary Rainford
Gary Sandland
Gary Shaw (Malaysia)
Gary Sutton
Gary William Sandywell
Gavin Hunter
Gavin Scott
Geoff Lawton
Geoff Platt
George (d) & Louise Wong
George Bose
George Gannon
George Lambert
George McCrae (USA)
Geraint Williams
Gerry Monty
Gerry Thomas (d)
Gill Black
Gillian & Brian Potter Merrigan
Gina Johnson
Gina Zubiena
Glen Thomas
Glynn Jones
Godwin Toner (Malta)
Gordon & Ronnie Ellison (d)
Graham & Fran John
Graham & Lynn Pitt
Graham Lawson
Graham Logan
Graham Norman
Graham Norton
Graham White
Greg & Tracey Wilson
Grega & Maria Rodger
Guido Demarco, President of Malta (d)
Guy Morris

Gwen Dickie
Gwen Harrison
Gwilym & Hywel Roberts (d)

H

Haley Olszewski (USA)
Harry & Eva Millington
Harry Barnes
Harry Shone
Hassan Sharter (d)
Heather Salmon
Helen & Paul Meacock
Helen Hibbert
Helen Miles
Helen Wow Flowers
Helga Marsh (d)
Hillary Roberts (f) (d)
Howard Turley
Hugh Chase

I

Ian & Irene Morris
Ian & Lorraine Ellison
Ian & Lyn McGuiness
Ian & Sheila (d) Kelsey
Ian & Wendy Cowell
Ian Bladon
Ian Bradshaw
Ian Calvert
Ian Dee
Ian Gordon
Ian Kendrick
Ian Longden (Singapore)
Ian Mason
Ian Pittman
Ian Robbins
Ian Woods
Icy Williams

Ikem Billy
Ina Hammer (Singapore)
Iris & Bobby (d) Johnson
Isobel Pearson
Isobel Richards
Ivan Mallia

J

Jack Nuttall
Jackie Pritchard
Jacky Finnigan Key 103
Jacqueline Giordmaina (Malta)
James Byrne
James Vost
James Whale
Jamie & Sarah Bates (f)
Jamie Briers (Equity)
Jamie McDonald (Australia)
Jamie Muir
Jan & Lyn Capper
Jane Dean
Jane Ritson
Janet Harris (Amsterdam)
Jan Probert
Jase & Jo Paton
Jay Alan Bates (f)
Jay Derricot
Jean & Dougy (d) Galtress
Jean Paul Mifsud (Malta)
Jeanette Stevens (USA)
Jean-Luc Saquet (France)
Jeff & Louise Norris
Jegsy Dodd
Jenny Jazz (Australia)
Jerry & Wilma Maynard (USA)
Jim & Denise Cubbon (I.O.M.)
Jim & Irene Wall

Jimmy Coultard
Jo & Elizabeth Bates (f) (d)
Joe & Amy Inch
Joe Power
Joe Vella (Malta)
Joe White (Bali)
John & Amanda Williams
John & Carlie Roberts (f)
John & Julie O Grady
John & Kate Bates (f)
John & Kerry Hodgekinson
John & Linda Denton
John & Marie Poole (f)
John & Max Cecchini
John & Sheila Birchall
John & Sheila Moffatt
John Barrow
John Bonner
John Caddo
John Collier
John Cummins
John Dolphin
John Gayton
John Griffiths
John Harding
John Hazlehurst
John Hilliyard
John Humphries
John Jessop
John Jones
John Klemmer (USA)
John Maguire (d)
John Mallan
John Meadows
John Newton
John Peers

John Peters
John Proctor
John Roberts
John Roscoe
John Sparke (d)
John Steven Locke
John, Christina & Hughna Cotton
John, Iris & Philip Broster
Jon Samuel
Jon Williams
Jonathan Chase
Jonathon Atherton (Australia)
Jono Windred (Bali)
Jorinde Williams
Joseph & Mary Mallia (Malta)
Josette Bartolo (Malta)
Josh & Holly Inch
Julia Elms
Julian Elmore
Julie Hodgeson
Justine Fairclough
K
Karen Burns
Karen & Melvin Buckley
Karen Cullen
Karen Melville
Karen Nolan Guy (d)
Karen Pickford
Karen Roberts (f)
Karl Bugeja (Malta)
Karl Mallia
Kathy Cote (USA)
Kay Diamond (d)
Keira Robyn Bates (f)
Keith & Dave Sterling
Keith & Nicky Scott

Keith (d) & Rita McCombe
Keith McCombe Jr
Keith Molineux
Keith Resness
Keith Stevens
Ken (d) & Jean Weston
Ken Davies
Ken Diamond
Ken Eaton
Ken Isherwood
Ken Webster
Kenneth Zammit Tabona (Malta)
Kenny James
Kenny Piper
Kenny Wilson (N. Ireland)
Kent Rees (Canada)
Kerry & Karin Ball (Bali)
Kev Seed
Kevin Burrows
Kevin Fishwick
Kevin Hackett
Kevin Walton
Khai Tyson (Singapore)
Kiki Billy Howe (d)
Kim & Steve Davies
Kim Sayce
Kim Woodburn
Kirk Farrell
Kitty Abbot
L
Lambert Fletcher (d)
Larry Byrne
Lee Brennan
Lee Butler
Lee Green
Lee Leung

Leigh Carrol (d)
Leighton Williams
Len Taylor (d)
Lenny & Mary (d) Barclay (USA)
Leo Rabbett (d)
Les Calvert
Les Cope (d)
Leslie Chrishop J.P.
Leslie Lees (USA)
Leslie Shallcross
Linda & Alan (d) Hornby
Linda Belsito (USA)
Linda Briggs
Linda Roberts
Lindsey Richards / Hare
Lionel Piper RAF VR (d)
Lisa Barnes
Lisa Rimmer
Lorraine Beauchamp (Canada)
Lorraine Taylor
Louise Christian
Louise Emerick
Louise Travis Jones
Lynne Rooney
M
Mac McNair - Booth
Mal & Gail (Kuala Lumpur)
Mal Thorey
Mandy Corrigan
Marc Oberon
Marcette Busuttil (Malta)
Maria & Colin Dennett
Maria Medium
Mariella Scerri (Malta)
Mark & Carl Brundell
Mark Blakemore

Mark Davis
Mark Nuttall
Mark Robinson (Canada)
Mark Simon
Marthese Mallia (Malta)
Martin & Wayne Giles
Martin Ellis
Martin Higgins
Martin Sapiano (Malta)
Martin Taylor
Mary Hooley (Equity)
Mary Rose (Malta)
Mary Simmons (f)
Matt Healey
Matthew & Melanie Toner (Malta)
Matty Jubb
Mavis & Brian Sadler (Australia)
Mavis Beckerleg (f)
May Medium
Megan Disberry
Mel (d) & Kim
Melanie Silver
Mel Lacey
Melissa & Rubin Roberts (f)
Michael Gannon
Michael Platt
Michael Preston
Michael Riake
Michael Salousti (Cyprus)
Michelle & Jono Dodd
Michelle Andrews
Mick Thomas
Mike & Ann Jones
Mike & Lynn Simmons
Mike Boyd
Mike Brereton

Mike Burgess
Mike Coburn
Mike Gibbons
Mike Hammond
Mike Hannigan
Mike J. Fox
Mike Lewis
Mike Lincoln
Mike Mally
Mike Morris (f)
Mike Rice
Mike Robbins
Mike Tudor
Mike White
Mike, Dee & Phil McCabe
Miray Williams
Mo Buckley
Mr (d) & Mrs Nair (Singapore)
Mugs Murray
N
Natalie Bodell
Natasha De Alwis (Kuala Lumpur)
Nathan Farrugia (Malta)
Neal & Clare Atkinson
Neil & Julie McNay
Neil & Kay Scott
Neil & Rachel Woods
Neil Elias
Neil Greaves (d)
Neil James
Neil Jones
Neil Morris
Neil Nuance
Nella Bencini (Malta)
Nic & Maxine Wilty
Nick & Sarah Deplidge

Nick Goodman
Nick Laverick
Nick Pope (Mod)
Nicky Ellis Pagan
Nicky Rushton
Nicola Ireland
Nicola Jane Johnson
Nicola Roberts
Nicola Saverimutto
Nigel & Nell Brown
Nigel Green (Malaysia)
Nigel J. Piper
Nikki Swan
Noel Harrison
Oz & Jay X.F.M (Malta)
P
P.J. Vassallo Mintoff (Malta)
Palace Hotel Sliema (Malta)
Parkgate Lodge 7263
Pat & Sid (d) Morris (f)
Pat Dickinson
Pat Molloy
Patrick Snell (Sky TV)
Patsy Martin
Patsy Simmons (f)
Paul & Angie Brown
Paul & Debbie Wookey
Paul & Faye Reynolds (Ibiza)
Paul & Helen Meacock
Paul & Jess Wise
Paul & Julie ENT UK
Paul & Kristina Pisani (Malta)
Paul Bernard (Denmark)
Paul Boardman
Paul Brennan
Paul Chase

Paul Clucus
Paul Connelly
Paul Conway
Paul Daniels
Paul Debek
Paul Dickinson
Paul Fell
Paul Flanagan
Paul Grice
Paul Highton
Paul Inch
Paul James
Paul Johnson (Singapore)
Paul Leslie Williams
Paul Lowrie-Clarkson
Paul Mini SMC
Paul Orman
Paul Sandman
Paul Saunders
Paul Wilson
Paul Woodsy Woods
Paul, Freddie & Ashleigh Nolan
Paula Griffiths
Pauline & Albert (d) McGovern
Pauline Attard (Malta)
Pauline Murphy
Peppe (d) & Fran Antonini
Peppi & Mandy Azzopardi (Malta)
Pete Balshaw
Pete Carrol
Peter & Maureen Makin
Peter Baragwanath
Peter Casson (d)
Peter Chadwick
Peter Chan
Peter Citrene

Peter Dixon
Peter Elvie
Peter Horsley
Peter John McKay
Peter Kay
Peter McQuarrie
Peter Millar
Peter Thomas (d)
Petra Bauernfeind (Germany)
Pez & Jacky Tellit
Phil & Hazel Archer Jones
Phil & Peter Williams
Phil Cahill (USA)
Phil Daemon
Phil Jones (d)
Phil Mathews
Phil McGraa
Philip Fava (Malta)
Phillip Jones
Phillip Kerr
Princess Hamidah (Brunei)
Q
Quill Potter (Mumbai)
R
Radio City Liverpool
Ralph E. Parsons
Ray & Shelagh (d) Goldstone
Ray Hunt
Ray Seabourne (d)
Reverend Andrew Dean (d)
Richard & Jeanette Fearnley Smith
Richard Spencer
Richie Piper
Rick Houghton
Rick Vaughn
Ricky Kirby

Ricky Moore
Ricky Tomlinson
Rob & Lorna Doyle
Rob Berriman
Rob Carter
Rob, Keira & Claudia Taylor
Robbie Edwards
Robbie Jones (d)
Robbie Robinson
Robbo & Ricey
Robert Egan
Robyn Cartwright (d)
Rod Holbrook
Roger & Nicola Davies
Roger (d) & Silvia Copson
Rolf Nuttall
Ron & Joan Balshaw
Ron (d) & Margret Cuthbert
Ronnie & Paul Hancock
Ronnie (d) & Jacky James
Ronnie Clucus (d)
Ronnie Gibbs (Canada)
Ronnie McDonald (d)
Ronnie Page (d)
Rose Marie Cassar (Malta)
Roy Basnett
Roy Teece
Roy Whigham (d)
Royston Mayoh
Russell & Tracey Burke
Russell White
S
Sachin Gopalan (Jakarta)
Sally Copson
Sam Radcliff
Sammy J. (Australia)

Sandra Davis (Malta)
Sandra Platt (d)
Sandy & Angie Holms
Sandy Postman
Sandy White (USA)
Sarah & Dave Ellis
Sarah & Mark Hope
Sarah Dawson
Sarah Morris
Saturday Night Boys (Staffs)
Scott E. Ellis (USA)
Sean & Jo Trimble
Seema Subash (Malaysia)
Seren Adelaide Bates (f)
Serrie & Gary Daengsvang
Seth Walmsley
Sharman Ali
Sharon & Steve Thomas
Sharon Boyd
Shaun Wood
Sheila & Brian McKeown (f)
Sid & Marge Walton (d)
Sid Cox (d)
Sidney Spencer RAF. DFC (d)
Simon Edwards
Simon Jackson
Simon Leung
Simon Mayo
Simon Munsrley
Simon Wells
Simone Backhouse
Sonia Coppen (d)
Southern Club Games
Staff & Ida Leitch
Stan Boardman
Stan Curry

Stan Moffatt
Steph Bates
Stephen Joseph (Malaysia) (d)
Stephen Moss
Steve & Andy Garry
Steve & Debbie Morris (f)
Steve & John Kennedy
Steve & Lynn Flanagan
Steve & Melanie Parry
Steve & Ruth Williams
Steve & Theresa McGregor
Steve (Cocky) Laycock
Steve Brolin
Steve Burkhill
Steve Coltrain
Steve Croft
Steve Elmore
Steve Harding
Steve Heath
Steve Johnson
Steve Kewley
Steve Lamatina
Steve McBride
Steve McKay
Steve McKenna
Steve Mera
Steve Molloy
Steve Murphy
Steve Phelan (Dubai)
Steve Sale
Steve Sault
Steve Stead
Steve Walton
Steve Wright
Steven Hinton
Stevie Banks

Stevie Star
Stuart Bernard
Stuart McNeil
Stuart Micallef (Malta)
Stuart Murdoch
Stuart Murphy
Stuart Swaine
Sue & Julie Hunter
Sue Roberts (f)
Sunny Hemrajani (India)
Susan Chadwick
Suzanne, Ivarna & Mario Schembri (Malta)
Sylvia Cartwright
T
Ted Jamieson (d)
Terry Lennaine
Terry Platt
The Blakemore's
Therese Mallia (Malta)
Thomas Arwel Ellis
Tim Johnson (Equity)
Tim Players-Lounge
Tim Sheard
Tina Chan
Tishman
Tom & Sue Flanagan
Tom & Val McCarten
Tom Ainscough (d)
Tom Bennett
Tom Pepper
Tom Rhodes (USA)
Tommy Burns
Tommy Smyth
Toni Roberts
Tonio & Jennifer Mallia (Malta)
Tony & Alison (d) Statham

Tony & Jillian Roberts
Tony & Jo Coburn
Tony & Joy James
Tony & Marni Howarth
Tony Mason
Tony Rae
Tony Reed
Tony Sands
Tony Tee
Tony Wilson (d)
Tony, Nat & Esmé Doyle
Tracey Buxton
Tracey Ryan
Trevor Courtnell
Trevor Howard (d)
Trevor M
Trix D.J.
Trixie Dog
Tsoi & Dan Leung
U
UTV World Movies
V
Val Atmosphere
Vernetta Lopez (Singapore)
Vijay Nair (Singapore)
Vince Williams
Vinny O'Connor (CNN)
Viv Worsley
Vivian Brown (d)
W
Weasel
Wee Willie DJ
Wilf & Heather Pavlak
Will & Sandra Bridson
Willy Millar
Wynne & Linda Roberts

X
Xarabank TV (Malta)
Y
Yousef Mohamed

Made in the USA
Charleston, SC
11 August 2015